# GoodFood
## Healthy chicken
## recipes

10 9 8 7 6 5 4 3 2 1

Published in 2014 by BBC Books, an imprint of Ebury Publishing
A Random House Group company

Photographs © BBC Worldwide 2014
Recipes © BBC Worldwide 2014
Book design © Woodlands Books Ltd 2014
All recipes contained in this book first appeared in BBC *Good Food* magazine.

The Random House Group Limited
Reg. No. 954009

Addresses for companies within the Random House Group can be found at www.randomhouse.co.uk

A CIP catalogue record for this book is available from the British Library

The Random House Group Limited supports the Forest Stewardship Council® (FSC®), the leading
international forest-certification organisation. Our books carrying the FSC label are printed on
FSC®-certified paper. FSC is the only forest-certification scheme supported by the leading
environmental organisations, including Greenpeace. Our paper procurement policy can be found at
www.randomhouse.co.uk/environment

To buy books by your favourite authors and register for offers visit www.randomhouse.co.uk

Printed and bound by Firmengruppe APPL, aprinta druck, Wemding, Germany
Colour origination by Dot Gradations Ltd, UK

Project Editor: Lizzy Gaisford
Designer: Kathryn Gammon
Production: Rebecca Jones
Picture Researcher: Gabby Harrington

ISBN: 9781849907835

MIX
Paper from
responsible sources
FSC
www.fsc.org    FSC® C004592

## Picture credits

BBC *Good Food* magazine and BBC Books would like to thank the following people for providing photos. While every effort has
been made to trace and acknowledge all photographers, we should like to apologies should there be any errors or omissions.

Iain Bagwell p51; Carolyn Barber p91; Steve Baxter p63; Peter Cassidy p17, p85, p149, p151; Charlie Richards p47, p137; Will Heap
p13, p31, p87, p97, p121, p155, p157, p169, p193, p209, p183, p191, p207; Amanda Heywood p37; Lara Holmes p25, p79, p81, p139;
Jonathan Kennedy p131, p161; Adrian Lawrence; Francine Lawrence p99;  p185; William Lingwood p61; Gareth Morgans p43, p59,
p111, p123; David Munns p11, p27, p45, p53, p75, p77, p83, p109, p105, p93, p95, p101, p117, p153, p159, p165, p181, p189, p199,
p201, p203 ; Myles New p19, p21, p23, p115, p127, p173; Stuart Ovenden p119, p175, p187; Lis Parsons p15, p33, p35, p39, p49, p55,
p57, p135, p147, p171, p197, p211; Craig Robertson p67, p73; Howard Shooter p89; Sam Stowell p69, p71, p113, p125, p129, p143,
p145, p163, p177, p179; Rob Streeter p41, p65; Yuki Sugiura p29; Dawie Verwey p141; Philip Webb p107; Simon Wheeler p195; Jon
Whitaker p103; Elizabeth Zeschin p133, p167, p205

All the recipes in this book were created by the editorial team at *Good Food* and by regular contributors to BBC magazines.

# healthy GoodFood
## Healthy chicken recipes

Editor **Barney Desmazery**

# Contents

# Introduction

At *Good Food* we pride ourselves on delivering you the recipes you're looking for and whenever we do any surveys the two key words that always appear at the top of the list are 'chicken' & 'healthy'.

So, sticking to our promise we thought it was time we brought you our collection of our favourite healthy chicken recipes – some of these are low in fat, some are low in calories, others are all-round healthy and packed with vegetables, and lastly there are a few classics that have had a makeover to make them altogether healthier than the original recipe.

Chicken is one of the most versatile ingredients around, which is why we all like it so much, but what this little book sets out to prove is that it can play its part in a healthy diet without you having to compromise on flavour or satisfaction.

Barney Desmazery

# Notes and conversion tables

NOTES ON THE RECIPES
- Eggs are large in the UK and Australia and extra large in America unless stated otherwise.
- Wash fresh produce before preparation.
- Recipes contain nutritional analyses for 'sugar', which means the total sugar content including all natural sugars in the ingredients, unless otherwise stated.

OVEN TEMPERATURES

| Gas | °C | °C Fan | °F | Oven temp. |
|---|---|---|---|---|
| ¼ | 110 | 90 | 225 | Very cool |
| ½ | 120 | 100 | 250 | Very cool |
| 1 | 140 | 120 | 275 | Cool or slow |
| 2 | 150 | 130 | 300 | Cool or slow |
| 3 | 160 | 140 | 325 | Warm |
| 4 | 180 | 160 | 350 | Moderate |
| 5 | 190 | 170 | 375 | Moderately hot |
| 6 | 200 | 180 | 400 | Fairly hot |
| 7 | 220 | 200 | 425 | Hot |
| 8 | 230 | 210 | 450 | Very hot |
| 9 | 240 | 220 | 475 | Very hot |

APPROXIMATE WEIGHT CONVERSIONS
- All the recipes in this book list both imperial and metric measurements. Conversions are approximate and have been rounded up or down. Follow one set of measurements only; do not mix the two.
- Cup measurements, which are used by cooks in Australia and America, have not been listed here as they vary from ingredient to ingredient. Kitchen scales should be used to measure dry/solid ingredients.

*Good Food* is concerned about sustainable sourcing and animal welfare. Where possible humanely reared meats, sustainably caught fish (see fishonline. org for further information from the Marine Conservation Society) and free-range chicken and eggs are used when recipes are originally tested.

SPOON MEASURES

Spoon measurements are level unless otherwise specified.

• 1 teaspoon (tsp) = 5ml
• 1 tablespoon (tbsp) = 15ml
• 1 Australian tablespoon = 20ml (cooks in Australia should measure 3 teaspoons where 1 tablespoon is specified in a recipe)


APPROXIMATE LIQUID CONVERSIONS

| metric | imperial | AUS | US |
| --- | --- | --- | --- |
| 50ml | 2fl oz | ¼ cup | ¼ cup |
| 125ml | 4fl oz | ½ cup | ½ cup |
| 175ml | 6fl oz | ¾ cup | ¾ cup |
| 225ml | 8fl oz | 1 cup | 1 cup |
| 300ml | 10fl oz/½ pint | ½ pint | 1¼ cups |
| 450ml | 16fl oz | 2 cups | 2 cups/1 pint |
| 600ml | 20fl oz/1 pint | 1 pint | 2½ cups |
| 1 litre | 35fl oz/1¾ pints | 1¾ pints | 1 quart |

# Chicken tikka rice salad

*Make this salad for a crowd or keep it in the fridge for a household to graze on over a busy weekend.*

**TAKES 40 MINUTES ● SERVES 6–8**

500g bag long grain rice
1 tsp turmeric powder
1 tsp medium curry powder
small bunch coriander, leaves roughly
    chopped, stalks reserved
100g bag toasted cashew nuts, ½ very
    roughly chopped
1 cucumber, deseeded and chopped
    into chunks
1 large red onion, finely chopped
about 110g pack pomegranate seeds
400g can black beans, drained and
    rinsed
2 x about 130g packs cooked chicken
    tikka pieces, chopped
natural yogurt and mini poppadum
    crisps, to serve (optional)

**FOR THE DRESSING**

4 tbsp mango chutney
1 tbsp sunflower oil
1 tbsp brown sugar
1 tbsp medium curry powder
juice 1½–2 lemons (depending on size)

**1** Cook the rice according to the pack instructions but add the turmeric and 1 teaspoon curry powder to the cooking water. Drain well and spread on a baking sheet lined with kitchen paper to cool.
**2** Meanwhile, finely chop the coriander stalks and whisk with all the dressing ingredients, plus 50ml seasoning.
**3** Tip the rice into a big mixing bowl. Using a fork, break up any large lumps, then mix in the cashews, cucumber, onion, coriander leaves, pomegranate seeds, beans and chicken. Pour over the dressing and lightly stir in, then cover and keep in the fridge. Eat over the next 2 days (as long as it's within the chicken use-by date). Keep a big spoon in the bowl so kids can easily help themselves. Top with a dollop of yogurt and add a handful of poppadum crisps, if you like.

PER SERVING (8) 473 kcals, protein 20g, carbs 76g, fat 9g, sat fat 2g, fibre 5g, sugar 15g, salt 0.4g

# Vietnamese chicken baguette (Báhn Mi)

*Save money and be the envy of all your colleagues by taking this on-trend sandwich to work in your lunchbox.*

**TAKES 1 HOUR • MAKES 1**

1 small boneless chicken breast
1 tsp olive oil
1 tsp rice vinegar
½ tsp golden caster sugar
juice ½ lime
½ small carrot, peeled and grated
2 spring onions, thinly sliced
2.5cm/1in piece cucumber, deseeded
  and sliced
½ red chilli, thinly sliced into rounds
1 sandwich baguette
3–4 Little Gem leaves, washed
1–2 tbsp sweet chilli sauce, to serve

**1** Put the chicken breast between two pieces of cling film and bash with a rolling pin to about 1cm/½in thick. Heat a griddle pan until hot. Rub the chicken with the oil, cook for 2–3 minutes per side, or until cooked through. Set aside to cool.

**2** Mix together the rice vinegar, sugar and lime juice, stirring until the sugar is dissolved. Add the carrot, spring onions, cucumber and chilli.

**3** Split a sandwich baguette along the top. Stuff with the Little Gem leaves and shred the chicken on top. Pile on the carrot mixture and wrap or put in a plastic box. Put the sweet chilli sauce in a small portable pot and when it's time for lunch, pour over the sauce just before tucking in.

PER BAGUETTE 439 kcals, protein 32g, carbs 61g, fat 7g, sat fat 1g, fibre 5g, sugar 18g, salt 1.6g

# Chicken & spring-onion wraps

*To make these wraps even healthier, search out wholegrain or multi-seed tortillas and use a nutritious leaf like watercress.*

**TAKES 5 MINUTES** ● **SERVES 4**

2 tbsp reduced-fat mayonnaise
2 tbsp green pesto sauce
4 curly lettuce leaves
250g/9oz cooked chicken breast, shredded
6 spring onions, shredded
12cm/4 ½in chunk cucumber, shredded
4 flour tortillas

**1** Thoroughly mix together the mayonnaise and pesto in a small bowl.
**2** Divide the lettuce leaves, chicken, spring onions and cucumber among the tortillas. Drizzle over the pesto dressing, roll up, cut in half and eat.

PER SERVING 267 kcals, protein 24g, carbs 25g, fat 9g, sat fat 2g, fibre 2g, sugar 3g, salt 1.62g

# Vitality chicken salad with avocado dressing

*A quick and easy lunch salad for one; if you can't find soya beans use frozen broad beans or peas instead.*

**TAKES 10 MINUTES • SERVES 1, EASILY DOUBLED**

handful frozen soya beans

1 skinless boneless cooked chicken breast, shredded

¼ cucumber, peeled, deseeded and chopped

½ avocado, flesh scooped out

few drops Tabasco sauce

juice ½ lemon, plus a lemon wedge to garnish

2 tsp extra virgin olive oil

5–6 Little Gem leaves

1 tsp mixed seeds

**1** Cook the soya beans in a pan of boiling water for 3 minutes. Rinse in cold water and drain thoroughly. Put the chicken, beans and cucumber in a bowl.

**2** Blitz the avocado, Tabasco, lemon juice and oil in a food processor or with a hand blender until smooth. Season, pour into the bowl and mix well to coat.

**3** Spoon the mixture into each of the lettuce leaves (or serve it alongside them) and sprinkle with the seeds. Chill until lunch, then garnish with a lemon wedge.

PER SERVING 433 kcals, protein 35g, carbs 6g, fat 28g, sat fat 6g, fibre 7g, sugar 4g, salt 0.2g

# Chicken & pasta salad

*Eat straight away as a pasta dish in its own right or leave to go cold and enjoy as a summery pasta salad.*

**TAKES 30 MINUTES** ● **SERVES 4**

1 red pepper, deseeded and thickly
   sliced
1 red onion, thickly sliced
1 tbsp olive oil
300g/10oz penne or fusilli pasta
4 boneless skinless chicken breasts
2 tbsp each chopped thyme and
   oregano leaves
pinch dried chilli flakes
2 garlic cloves, crushed
150g pack cherry tomatoes, halved
50g bag rocket leaves
1 tbsp white wine vinegar

**1** Heat oven to 220C/200C fan/gas 7. Mix the pepper and onion with 1 teaspoon of the oil and roast for 20 minutes. Set aside.

**2** Cook the pasta according to the pack instructions. Drain and set aside.

**3** Meanwhile, put the chicken breasts between two sheets of cling film and bash with a rolling pin until they're about 1cm/½in thick. Mix the remaining oil, herbs, chilli and garlic then rub all over the chicken. Heat a griddle or barbecue and cook for 3–4 minutes on each side.

**4** Slice the chicken on a board, scrape into the pasta with any juices, plus the roasted onion and pepper, the cherry tomatoes, rocket, vinegar and some seasoning. Toss together and eat warm or cold.

PER SERVING 470 kcals, protein 44g, carbs 64g, fat 6g, sat fat 1g, fibre 4g, sugar 7g, salt 0.26g

# Chicken soba noodles

*A tip to stop noodles from overcooking for this trendy packed lunch is to drain them then cool them under cold running water.*

**TAKES 20 MINUTES • SERVES 1**

85g/3oz bundle soba or buckwheat
   noodles
small drizzle sesame oil
8 mangetout
1 small carrot
½ red chilli
1 tbsp toasted sesame seeds
handful shredded cooked chicken
soy sauce, to serve

**1** Cook the noodles according to the pack instructions, drain well, cool under cold water and drain again, then tip into a bowl and toss with a small drizzle of sesame oil.
**2** Finely slice the mangetout, cut the carrot into matchsticks and deseed and slice the red chilli. Add the vegetables and chilli to the noodles with the toasted sesame seeds and the shredded cooked chicken. Pack into a plastic container with a small portion of soy sauce to drizzle over just before eating.

PER SERVING 495 kcals, protein 29g, carbs 68g, fat 12g, sat fat 2g, fibre 6g, sugar 7g, salt 2.1g

# Cranberry-chicken salad

*If you want to make this simple salad more substantial, add a 400g can of drained and rinsed cannellini beans.*

**TAKES 25 MINUTES • SERVES 4**

2 boneless skinless chicken breasts
4 tsp olive oil
2 red onions, thinly sliced
200g/7oz mixed leaves
½ cucumber, deseeded and sliced
25g/1oz dried cranberries
85g/3oz cranberry sauce
juice 1 lime

**1** Slice each chicken breast in half horizontally to give four thin breasts, then rub with half the oil and season. Heat a non-stick frying pan and fry the chicken for 3 minutes on each side until cooked through. Set aside on a plate.

**2** Heat the remaining oil in the pan and fry the onions for 5 minutes. Slice the chicken, collecting any juices, and layer up with the onions, leaves, cucumber and dried cranberries. Mix together the cranberry sauce, lime juice, 2 tablespoons water and any chicken resting juices, and drizzle over the salad.

PER SERVING 190 kcals, protein 18g, carbs 19g, fat 5g, sat fat 1g, fibre 2g, sugar 17g, salt 0.12g

# Chicken, pea guacamole & radish wrap

*Whether you're after a lunchbox filler or need a new idea for a post-workout snack, this prepare-ahead wrap will stop you grabbing something unhealthy.*

**TAKES 5 MINUTES • SERVES 1**

50g/2oz cold cooked peas
2 tbsp low-fat soft cheese
a little lemon zest and juice
1 reduced-salt tortilla wrap
50g/2oz cooked boneless skinless
    chicken breast, sliced
2–3 radishes, sliced

**1** Use a fork to crush the peas together with the soft cheese in a bowl to make a chunky spread then stir in the lemon zest and juice, and season.

**2** Spread the crushed peas over the wrap and top with a thick layer of chicken and radishes. Roll up tightly and keep in the fridge until ready to eat, then cut in half to serve.

PER SERVING 336 kcals, protein 29g, carbs 32g, fat 10g, sat fat 4g, fibre 7g, sugar 4g, salt 1.2g

# Miso brown rice & chicken salad

*Not only is brown rice healthier than white it has a nuttier flavour and texture too, ideal when used in prepare-ahead salads like this.*

**TAKES 40 MINUTES • SERVES 2**

100g/4oz brown basmati rice
2 boneless skinless chicken breasts
140g/5oz purple sprouting broccoli
4 spring onions, diagonally sliced
1 tbsp toasted sesame seeds

**FOR THE DRESSING**

2 tsp miso paste
1 tbsp rice vinegar
1 tbsp mirin
1 tsp grated ginger

**1** Cook the rice according to the pack instructions, then drain and keep warm. Meanwhile, put the chicken breasts in a pan of boiling water so they are completely covered. Boil for 1 minute, then turn off the heat, put on a lid and let sit for 15 minutes. When cooked through, cut into slices.

**2** Boil the broccoli until tender. Drain, rinse under cold water and drain again. To make the dressing, mix the miso, rice vinegar, mirin and ginger together.

**3** Divide the rice between two plates and scatter over the spring onions and sesame seeds. Put the broccoli and chicken slices on top. To finish, drizzle over the dressing.

PER SERVING 419 kcals, protein 39g, carbs 53g, fat 7g, sat fat 1g, fibre 5g, sugar 4g, salt 0.76g

# Thai shredded chicken & runner-bean salad

*Enjoy this flavour-packed seasonal salad on its own, with rice or as part of a buffet with other salads.*

**TAKES 35 MINUTES ● SERVES 4**

200g/7oz runner beans, topped and tailed
1 red chilli, halved, deseeded and finely sliced, use 1 bird's-eye chilli, for more heat
2 shallots, finely sliced
1 lemongrass stalk, finely sliced
2cm/¾in piece ginger, shredded
2 cooked boneless skinless chicken breasts
small bunch mint leaves
large bunch Thai basil or coriander
1 lime, cut into wedges or cheeks, to squeeze over
steamed jasmine rice, to serve

**FOR THE COCONUT DRESSING**

100ml/3½fl oz coconut cream
1 garlic clove, crushed
3 tbsp Thai fish sauce
1 tsp sugar
juice 1 lime
1 bird's-eye chilli, finely diced

**1** Run a potato peeler down either side of the beans to remove any stringy bits. Cut into strips using a bean slicer, or on the diagonal into 2cm/¾in pieces. Cook the beans in simmering salted water for 4 minutes or until tender but still bright green. Drain and put in a bowl with the chilli, shallots, lemongrass and ginger. Pull the chicken breasts into shreds using your fingers and add to the bowl.

**2** Make the dressing. Mix the coconut with the garlic, fish sauce, sugar, lime and chilli. Tear the mint and Thai basil or coriander over the chicken and toss everything together. Pile on to a plate and pour over the dressing. Serve with the lime to squeeze over and some jasmine rice.

PER SERVING 214 kcals, protein 23g, carbs 6g, fat 11g, sat fat 8g, fibre 1g, sugar 5g, salt 2.31g

# Chicken-noodle soup

*Comfort food without the calories. Give this soup an easy Asian twist by adding some shredded fresh ginger and a splash of soy sauce if you want.*

**TAKES 20 MINUTES • SERVES 4**

1.2 litres/2 pints low-sodium chicken stock
4 small carrots, peeled and chopped
140g/5oz medium egg noodles
200g/7oz shredded cooked chicken
200g/7oz frozen peas
1 bunch spring onions, sliced, white and green parts separated

**1** Bring the stock to the boil in a large pan and throw in the carrots. Boil for 4 minutes until just tender then add the noodles and simmer for 3 minutes until the noodles are cooked through.
**2** Stir in the chicken, peas and the white part of the spring onions, heat for 1 minute or until everything is hot through. Ladle into bowls and scatter with the green part of the spring onions to serve.

PER SERVING 285 kcals, protein 23g, carbs 36g, fat 6g, sat fat 1g, fibre 5g, sugar 6g, salt 0.42g

# Cumin-chicken & avocado salad

*Using spices like cumin as a seasoning is a great way of giving a dish lots of flavour without adding extra salt or fat.*

**TAKES 20 MINUTES • SERVES 4**

2 tbsp olive oil

1 heaped tsp ground cumin

1 heaped tsp mild chilli powder

4 skinless chicken breast fillets

400g pack cherry tomatoes, halved if large

1 red onion, finely chopped

4 Little Gem lettuce hearts, separated into leaves

20g pack coriander leaves, roughly chopped

3 Hass avocados, peeled and thickly sliced

2 tbsp Caesar dressing (ready-made is fine)

410g can red kidney beans, drained and rinsed

crusty bread or crunchy tortilla chips, to serve

**1** Mix the oil and spices in a large bowl, then use the mixture to coat the chicken. Pan-fry the chicken (without extra oil) in a large non-stick frying pan for a few minutes each side. Toss the tomatoes into any spiced oil left in the bowl, then add them to the pan. Cover and cook for 5 minutes more until the chicken is cooked and the tomatoes are warm and starting to soften.

**2** Meanwhile, toss the onion, lettuce, coriander and avocados in the Caesar dressing and pile on to a large platter. Top with small handfuls of the beans and scatter with the tomatoes. Slice the warm chicken and pile on top. Serve with crusty bread or crunchy tortilla chips.

PER SERVING 544 kcals, protein 39g, carbs 20g, fat 35g, sat fat 7g, fibre 10g, sugar 9g, salt 1g

# Curried-chicken & mango salad

*This share-with-a-friend light lunch is a healthier spin on the classic coronation chicken.*

**TAKES 40 MINUTES ● SERVES 2**

6 chicken mini fillets
1 tsp olive oil
2 tsp curry powder
4 tbsp Greek-style yogurt
2 tbsp mango chutney
zest ½ lime and 2 tsp juice
1 Little Gem lettuce, leaves separated
1 ripe mango, peeled and sliced
½ red onion, finely sliced
2 tsp toasted sesame seeds

**1** Heat oven to 200C/180C fan/gas 6. Toss the chicken in the oil and 1 teaspoon of the curry powder, season and mix well to coat. Put the chicken on a foil-lined baking sheet and bake for 20 minutes until cooked through. Leave to cool a little, then slice and set aside.
**2** Meanwhile, make the dressing. In a bowl, combine the remaining curry powder with the yogurt, chutney and lime zest and juice (add 1 tablespoon water if the dressing is a little thick).
**3** To serve, arrange the lettuce leaves on two plates. Top with the mango and cooked chicken, then drizzle with the dressing. Scatter with the red onion and sesame seeds before serving.

PER SERVING 453 kcals, protein 35g, carbs 43g, fat 15g, sat fat 7g, fibre 5g, sugar 41g, salt 0.9g

# Chicken & pepper pittas

*If you find raw peppers a little hard to digest try simply peeling them with a normal vegetable peeler first.*

**TAKES 25 MINUTES • SERVES 2**

1 tbsp olive oil

2 boneless skinless cooked chicken
   breasts, cut into strips

pinch chilli flakes

1 red and 1 yellow pepper, deseeded
   and cut into strips

3 spring onions, trimmed and sliced

1 avocado, stoned, peeled and sliced

handful coriander leaves

2 wholemeal pitta breads, toasted and
   halved to form pockets

2 tbsp soured cream

**1** Heat the oil in a wok or large frying pan and fry the chicken and chilli flakes for 5–6 minutes. Add the peppers and spring onions, and stir-fry until the chicken is cooked but the peppers still have crunch. Season.

**2** Divide the avocado and coriander among the pitta halves, then spoon in the chicken-and-pepper mix. Add a dollop of soured cream to each and serve straight away.

PER SERVING 526 kcals, protein 35g, carbs 45g, fat 24g, sat fat 5g, fibre 9g, sugar 11g, salt 1.05g

# Chicken & chickpea salad with curry-yogurt dressing

*Poaching chicken breasts rather than frying them not only cuts down on the fat but also keeps them more succulent.*

**TAKES 30 MINUTES ● SERVES 2**

2 boneless skinless chicken breasts
200g/7oz 0% fat Greek-style yogurt
2 tsp mild curry powder
juice ½ lemon
small handful mint leaves, most
    chopped
400g can chickpeas, drained and rinsed
100g/4oz cherry tomatoes, quartered
1 small red onion, chopped
1 tbsp peanuts, crushed

**1** Bring a pan of water to the boil. Add the chicken breasts and some salt, then put on the lid. Turn off the heat and leave for 15 minutes until cooked through. Drain and then shred the chicken.

**2** In a small bowl, mix the yogurt, curry powder, lemon juice, chopped mint and some seasoning.

**3** Toss the chicken and chickpeas with half the dressing and season. Arrange on two plates and scatter over the tomatoes, onion, remaining mint and the peanuts. Drizzle the rest of the dressing over the top.

PER SERVING 406 kcals, protein 50g, carbs 32g, fat 7g, sat fat 1g, fibre 7g, sugar 8g, salt 1.3g

# Five-a-day chicken couscous

*Cheap, easy and packed with vegetables – healthy solo suppers don't get much better than this.*

**TAKES 40 MINUTES • SERVES 1**

1 medium courgette, cut into small chunks
1 medium carrot, cut into small chunks
1 medium red onion, cut into wedges
85g/3oz mushrooms, quartered
handful cherry tomatoes (about 8)
2 garlic cloves, peeled
1 tbsp olive oil
½ tsp paprika
½ tsp dried chilli flakes
2 bone-in chicken thighs, skin on
50g/2oz couscous
½ small pack parsley or mint, roughly chopped
drizzle sweet chilli sauce (optional)

**1** Heat oven to 200C/180C fan/gas 6. Put the vegetables and garlic on a baking sheet. Season well, drizzle with 1 teaspoon of the olive oil and mix until everything is coated.

**2** Sprinkle the spices and some seasoning over the chicken thighs, then rub into the skin and flesh. Drizzle a little oil over the skin and nestle the thighs among the veg. Roast in the oven for 25–30 minutes until the vegetables are starting to crisp and the chicken is cooked through.

**3** About 10 minutes before the chicken and vegetables are done, put the couscous in a bowl and just cover with boiling water, then cover with cling film and set aside for 5 minutes.

**4** Fork through the couscous to separate the grains. Toss the vegetables and parsley or mint through the couscous, season, then transfer to a serving plate. Top with the chicken and drizzle over the sweet chilli sauce, if you like.

PER SERVING 725 kcals, protein 43g, carbs 54g, fat 36g, sat fat 8g, fibre 9g, sugar 18g, salt 0.9g

# Griddled chicken & corn salad

*The griddled elements to this summery salad could just as easily be cooked on the barbecue – weather permitting, of course.*

**TAKES 30 MINUTES • SERVES 4**

4 small boneless skinless chicken
   breasts
2 garlic cloves, crushed
1 tbsp paprika
juice 1 lemon
2 tbsp olive oil
2 corn cobs
4 Little Gem lettuces, quartered
   lengthways
½ cucumber, diced
your favourite dressing, to serve

**1** Cut the chicken breasts in half lengthways so you are left with eight chicken strips. Mix the garlic, paprika, lemon juice and 1 tablespoon of the oil with some seasoning, and toss with the chicken. Leave to marinate for at least 15 minutes.

**2** Heat a griddle pan, brush with half the remaining oil and cook the chicken for 3–4 minutes each side until cooked through. Brush the remaining oil over the corn cobs and griddle, turning to cook evenly, for about 5 minutes or until lightly charred. Remove and cut off the kernels.

**3** Mix the lettuce and cucumber on a platter, top with the corn kernels and chicken, and drizzle over your choice of dressing.

PER SERVING 236 kcals, protein 28g, carbs 12g, fat 8g, sat fat 1g, fibre 3g, sugar 4g, salt 0.2g

# Chicken, edamame & ginger pilaf

*If you can't find frozen edamame beans, frozen peas or broad beans will work just as well.*

**TAKES 30 MINUTES • SERVES 4**

2 tbsp vegetable oil
1 onion, thinly sliced
thumb-size piece ginger, grated
1 red chilli, deseeded and finely sliced
3 skinless chicken breasts, cut into
   bite-size pieces
250g/9oz basmati rice
600ml/1 pint vegetable stock
100g/4oz frozen edamame/soya beans
coriander leaves, to sprinkle
0% fat Greek-style yogurt (optional),
   to serve

**1** Heat the oil in a medium pan, then add the onion, ginger and chilli, along with some salt and pepper. Sizzle everything for 5 minutes until the onions are starting to soften. Add the chicken and the rice, and cook for 2 minutes more, then pour over the stock and bring to the boil.

**2** Turn the heat to low, cover and simmer gently for 8–10 minutes until the rice is just cooked. During the final 3 minutes of cooking, add the edamame beans. Sprinkle some coriander leaves on top and serve with a dollop of Greek yogurt, if you like.

PER SERVING 436 kcals, protein 32g, carbs 52g, fat 9g, sat fat 1g, fibre 3g, sugar 4g, salt 0.5g

# Chicken, red-pepper & almond traybake

*Here's everything you need for a well-balanced, flavoursome meal, all simply roasted together for ease.*

**TAKES 1 HOUR ● SERVES 4**

500g/1lb 2oz boneless skinless chicken thighs

3 medium red onions, cut into thick wedges

500g/1lb 2oz small red potatoes, cut into thick slices

2 red peppers, deseeded and cut into thick slices

1 garlic clove, finely chopped

1 tsp each ground cumin, smoked paprika and fennel seeds, slightly crushed

3 tbsp olive oil

zest and juice 1 lemon

50g/2oz whole blanched almonds, roughly chopped

170g tub 0% Greek-style yogurt

small handful parsley or coriander leaves, chopped, to garnish

**1** Heat oven to 200C/180C fan/gas 6. Put the chicken, onions, potatoes and peppers in a large bowl and season. In another bowl, mix together the garlic, spices, oil, and lemon zest and juice. Pour this over everything and spread the mixture between two baking sheets.

**2** Roast for 40 minutes, turning over after 20 minutes, until the chicken is cooked through. Add the almonds for the final 8 minutes of cooking. Serve in bowls with a big dollop of Greek yogurt and some chopped parsley or coriander sprinkled over.

---

PER SERVING 442 kcals, protein 34g, carbs 34g, fat 20g, sat fat 3g, fibre 5g, sugar 11g, salt 0.34g

# Korean rice pot

*This signature Korean dish, called bibimbap, consists of lots of different ingredients but will always contain rice topped with egg and served with chilli sauce.*

**TAKES 30 MINUTES • SERVES 4**

500ml/18fl oz hot chicken stock
250g/9oz long grain rice
300g/10oz boneless skinless cooked
   chicken, diced
250g/9oz baby leaf spinach
2 carrots, shredded
1 tsp toasted sesame oil
1 tsp toasted sesame seeds
2 tbsp vegetable oil
4 eggs
2 tbsp thick chilli sauce

**1** Pour the chicken stock into a large pan and bring to the boil. Add the rice and chicken, bring back to the boil and simmer for 12–15 minutes until the stock has been absorbed and the rice is tender.

**2** Meanwhile, put the spinach in a colander and pour over a kettle of hot water to lightly wilt, then squeeze out the water to drain. Keep the spinach and carrots separate, but dress both with the sesame oil and seeds.

**3** Cover the cooked rice with a lid and leave to sit for a couple of minutes. Meanwhile, heat the vegetable oil in a non-stick pan set over a high heat. Fry the eggs so the white crisps up nicely round the edges.

**4** Spoon the rice into large bowls and arrange the spinach and carrots on top. Finish each with a fried egg and a dollop of chilli sauce. Serve immediately.

PER SERVING 537 kcals, protein 39g, carbs 60g, fat 17g, sat fat 4g, fibre 3g, sugar 5g, salt 1.33g

# Speedy microwave leek & chicken hotpot

*Get more from your microwave with this quick and easy one pot – just make sure you serve it with bread rolls to mop up the delicious juices.*

**TAKES 30 MINUTES** ● **SERVES 4**

2 baking potatoes, peeled and cut into chunks

2 leeks, cut into thick slices and washed

3 medium carrots, peeled and cut into 3cm/1¼in slices

300ml/½ pint hot chicken stock

4 skinless boneless chicken breasts, diced

3 tbsp double cream

1 tbsp chopped parsley leaves

bread rolls, to serve

**1** Put the potatoes, leeks and carrots together in a shallow microwave-safe dish with some salt and pepper. Pour over the stock. Cover the dish with cling film and pierce a few times with the point of a knife. Cook on High for 10 minutes until the potatoes are just starting to become tender.

**2** Remove the dish from the microwave, peel off the cling film and stir in the chicken. Cover the dish with fresh cling film and pierce again, then cook on High for 6 minutes or until the chicken is cooked and succulent.

**3** Remove the dish from the microwave, uncover and stir in the cream and parsley plus black pepper to taste. Serve straight from the dish, with bread to mop up the juices.

PER SERVING 293 kcals, protein 36g, carbs 19g, fat 8g, sat fat 4g, fibre 4.6g, sugar 6g, salt 0.4g

# Mexican chicken & wild-rice soup

*Pouches of ready cooked rice make a great storecupboard standby. If you can't find the specific wild-rice mix for this recipe, any pouch or just home-cooked rice will do.*

**TAKES 30 MINUTES ● SERVES 4**

1 tsp olive oil
1 onion, finely chopped
1 green pepper, deseeded and diced
200g/7oz sweetcorn, frozen or from a can
1–2 tbsp chipotle paste
250g pouch ready cooked long grain and wild-rice mix or any ready cooked rice
400g can black beans in water, drained and rinsed
1.3 litres/2¼ pints low-sodium chicken stock
2 cooked boneless skinless chicken breasts, shredded
small bunch coriander, chopped
low-fat soured cream and reduced-fat guacamole, to garnish (optional)

**1** Heat the oil in a large non-stick frying pan and cook the onion for 5 minutes. Throw in the pepper and cook for 2 minutes more, then add the sweetcorn, chipotle paste and rice. Stir well and cook for 1–2 minutes.

**2** Add the black beans and the stock. Bring to the boil, turn down to a simmer, then add half the chicken and coriander. Cool for 2–3 minutes, then ladle into bowls.

**3** Scatter over the rest of the chicken and coriander. Serve with a dollop each of soured cream and guacamole on top, if you like.

PER SERVING 347 kcals, protein 29g, carbs 45g, fat 7g, sat fat 1g, fibre 5g, sugar 5g, salt 0.48g

# Chipotle chicken

*Chipotle paste is an easy way to give a dish authentic, smoky, Mexican flavours. Look for it in the world food aisle of larger supermarkets or buy it online.*

**TAKES 50 MINUTES • SERVES 4**

2 tbsp sunflower oil
1 onion, chopped
1 garlic clove, sliced
1–2 tbsp chipotle paste
400g can chopped tomatoes
1 tbsp cider vinegar
8 skinless chicken thigh fillets
small bunch coriander, chopped
soured cream and rice, to serve

**1** Heat the oil in a deep, wide frying pan and fry the onion and garlic gently for 10 minutes until soft. Add the chipotle paste (use 1 tablespoon for a mild flavour and 2 tablespoons for a hotter, stronger one). Stir and cook for 1 minute, then add the tomatoes and vinegar. Bring to a simmer and cook for 10 minutes with the lid half on. Stir to make sure it doesn't get too dry.
**2** Add the chicken and cook for 10 minutes or until cooked through, turning once. Scatter with coriander and serve with rice and soured cream.

PER SERVING 286 kcals, protein 42g, carbs 6g, fat 11g, sat fat 3g, fibre 2g, sugar 4g, salt 0.64g

# Chicken, potato & green-bean curry

*Always use full-fat yogurt when cooking as the low-fat versions are likely to curdle when added to hot sauces.*

**TAKES 40 MINUTES • SERVES 4**

1 tbsp sunflower oil
1 onion, chopped
6 skinless chicken thigh fillets, diced
2 potatoes, cut into small cubes
2 tbsp mild curry paste
500g/1lb 2oz tomato passata
200g/7oz fine green beans
150g pot full-fat natural yogurt
plain steamed rice or warm naan
    bread, to serve

**1** Heat the oil in a large frying pan and cook the onion and chicken together over a medium heat for 5 minutes until the onion is soft.

**2** Add the potatoes, curry paste and passata, bring to the boil, then cover and gently simmer for 15 minutes.

**3** Add the beans and a splash of water, and continue to cook for 10–15 minutes more until all the vegetables are tender and the chicken is cooked through. Remove from the heat and stir in the yogurt. Serve with rice or naan.

PER SERVING 333 kcals, protein 36g, carbs 26g, fat 10g, sat fat 3g, fibre 3g, sugar 10g, salt 1.34g

# Chicken-masala skewers

*Increase your daily vegetable count by adding chunks of courgette, cubes of pepper or onion wedges to the skewers.*

**TAKES 25 MINUTES • SERVES 4**

140g/5oz 0% fat Greek-style yogurt
2 tbsp masala curry paste
handful coriander leaves, chopped,
　　plus extra to garnish
juice 1 lime, pinch zest, plus wedges,
　　to garnish
4 skinless boneless chicken breasts,
　　each cut into 6 chunks
wholemeal chapatis, to serve

**FOR THE SALAD**

250g pack cherry tomatoes, halved or
　　quartered
1 red onion, finely chopped
1 cucumber, cut into chunks

**1** In a large bowl mix the yogurt, curry paste, half the chopped coriander, half the lime juice and all the zest. Tip in the chicken, stir to coat and leave in the fridge to marinate for 30 minutes, if you have time.

**2** Thread the chicken on to eight skewers and cook in batches on a hot griddle pan or barbecue, or in a frying pan, for about 10–12 minutes, turning until cooked through.

**3** Meanwhile, mix all of the salad ingredients with the remaining lime juice and coriander in a bowl and season. Sprinkle with extra coriander and serve alongside the skewers with warmed wholemeal chapatis.

PER SERVING 227 kcals, protein 39g, carbs 8g, fat 4g, sat fat 1g, fibre 2g, sugar 6g, salt 0.77g

# Chicken & white-bean stew

*This can be turned into a minestrone by doubling the stock and cutting the chicken finer and adding pasta.*

**TAKES 1 HOUR 20 MINUTES**

● **SERVES 4**

2 tbsp sunflower oil

400g/14oz boneless skinless chicken
   thighs, trimmed and cut into chunks

1 onion, finely chopped

3 carrots, finely chopped

3 celery sticks, finely chopped

2 thyme sprigs or ó tsp dried

1 bay leaf, fresh or dried

600ml/1 pint vegetable or chicken
   stock

2 x 400g cans haricot beans, drained
   and rinsed

handful chopped parsley, crusty bread,
   to serve

**1** Heat the oil in a large pan, add the chicken, then fry until lightly browned. Add the vegetables, then fry for a few minutes more. Stir in the herbs and stock. Bring to the boil. Stir well, reduce the heat, then cover and simmer gently for 40 minutes, until the chicken is tender.

**2** Stir the beans into the pan, then simmer for 5 minutes to heat them through. Stir in the parsley and serve with crusty bread.

---

PER SERVING 291 kcals, protein 30g, carbs 24g, fat 9g, sat fat 2g, fibre 11g, sugar 9g, salt 0.66g

# Crispy chicken & asparagus bake

*Make the most of the short British asparagus season with this easy-to-prepare crumb-topped bake.*

**TAKES 30 MINUTES • SERVES 4**

4 boneless skinless chicken breasts, cut into bite-size pieces
knob butter
100g/4oz asparagus, cut into bite-size pieces
100g/4oz green spring vegetables (we used baby leaf spinach and defrosted peas)
100g/4oz ham, torn
100ml/4fl oz low-fat crème fraîche
50g/2oz fresh breadcrumbs

**1** Heat grill to medium. Spread the chicken out evenly in a shallow baking dish. Dot with half the butter and grill for 7–10 minutes, turning occasionally until cooked through. Meanwhile, put the vegetables in a bowl and pour a kettle of boiling water over them. Leave for 2–3 minutes, then drain.

**2** Scatter the veg and ham over the chicken, dollop on the crème fraîche and season to taste. Sprinkle on the breadcrumbs, dot with the remaining butter, then slide under the grill for 5 minutes more until heated through and the topping is crisp.

PER SERVING 300 kcals, protein 43g, carbs 13g, fat 9g, sat fat 5g, fibre 1g, sugar none, salt 1.21g

# Chicken, kale and sprout stir fry

*Sprouts aren't just for Christmas, added to dishes like this they hold their own as well as any other healthy leafy-green vegetable.*

**TAKES 30 MINUTES ● SERVES 2**

100g/4oz soba noodles
100g/4oz shredded curly kale
2 tsp sesame oil
2 skinless boneless chicken breasts, sliced into thin strips
25g/1oz piece ginger, peeled and sliced into matchsticks
1 red pepper, deseeded and thinly sliced
handful Brussels sprouts, cut into quarters
1 tbsp low-sodium soy sauce
2 tbsp rice wine or white wine vinegar
zest and juice 1 lime

**1** Cook the noodles according to the pack instructions, then drain and set aside. Meanwhile, heat a large wok or frying pan and add the kale along with a good splash of water and cook for 1–2 minutes until wilted, with a little bite remaining, then cool under cold running water to keep the colour.

**2** Add half the oil to the wok or pan and cook the chicken strips until browned, then remove and set aside. Heat the remaining oil and fry the ginger, pepper and sprouts until softened a little. Return the chicken and kale to the pan and add the noodles.

**3** Tip in the soy, rice or white wine vinegar and lime zest and juice along with enough water to create a sauce that clings to the ingredients. Serve immediately.

PER SERVING 381 kcals, protein 36g, carbs 50g, fat 6g, sat fat 1g, fibre 5g, sugar 7g, salt 2.1g

# Spice & lime chicken

*This is great with low-fat, skinless boneless chicken breasts, but this tasty marinade would work just as well on barbecued chicken pieces or lamb chops.*

**TAKES 30 MINUTES, PLUS
MARINATING ● SERVES 4**

150g pot full-fat natural yogurt
1 tbsp vegetable oil
1 tsp medium curry powder or paste
pinch chilli powder
juice 1 lime
1 garlic clove, crushed
4 skinless boneless chicken breasts
1 red or green pepper, deseeded and
   cut into large chunks
1 onion, halved and cut into large
   chunks
steamed rice and ready-made raita,
   to serve

**1** Mix together the first six ingredients in a large bowl with some seasoning. Slash the chicken breasts lightly 5–6 times, without cutting all the way through. Add the chicken and vegetables to the yogurt mix, stir to coat, then marinate for 10 minutes.
**2** Put a griddle over a high heat, then cook the chicken and vegetables for 4 minutes each side. Leave to rest for 2 minutes before serving with steamed rice and raita.

PER SERVING 221 kcals, protein 36g, carbs 8g, fat 5g, sat fat 1g, fibre none, sugar none, salt 0.3g

# Chicken & cherry-tomato lentils

*Eating more pulses is a quick way to improve your diet, and it's never been easier now that there are so many pouches and canned varieties available.*

**TAKES 25 MINUTES • SERVES 4**

500g/1lb 2oz skinless boneless chicken
    thighs, cut into chunks
1 red onion, cut into wedges through
    the root
1 tbsp olive oil
200g/7oz cherry tomatoes
1 tbsp cumin seeds
2 x 250g pouches microwavable
    Puy lentils
2 tbsp red wine vinegar
handful parsley leaves, chopped

**1** Heat oven to 200C/180C fan/gas 6. Toss the chicken and onion with the oil, arrange on a baking sheet and season. Roast for 10 minutes, then add the cherry tomatoes and sprinkle over the cumin seeds. Cook for another 10 minutes.

**2** Meanwhile, heat the Puy lentils according to the pack instructions, then turn out into a large serving bowl. Once the chicken is ready, add everything to the bowl with the lentils and toss together. Stir in the vinegar, parsley and some seasoning to taste.

PER SERVING 356 kcals, protein 41g, carbs 31g, fat 9g, sat fat 2g, fibre 10g, sugar 5g, salt 1.7g

# Fragrant spiced chicken with banana sambal

*Chicken and banana may seem like an unusual pairing, but with the help of the right combination of spices it really works.*

**TAKES 1 HOUR • SERVES 6**

2 large onions, quartered

4 garlic cloves

thumb-size piece fresh ginger, peeled and roughly chopped

600ml/1 pint reduced-salt chicken stock

1 tsp each ground coriander and cumin

½ tsp turmeric powder

4 green cardamom pods

1 large fresh red chilli, deseeded and finely chopped

2 tbsp ground almonds

2 tbsp tomato purée

500g/1lb 2oz boneless skinless chicken breasts, cubed

small pack coriander, chopped

250g pack ready cooked brown basmati rice

**FOR THE SAMBAL**

1 small red onion, finely chopped

¼ cucumber, skinned, seeded and diced

1 small banana, diced

½ lime, grated zest and juice

**1** Put the onions in a food processor with the garlic and ginger. Blitz until smooth, pour in the stock and blitz again.

**2** Heat a large non-stick pan, sprinkle in the spices and toast for a minute. Pour in the onion mixture with 300ml/½ pint water and all but ½ teaspoon of the chopped chilli, plus the almonds and tomato purée, and stir well. Cover and simmer for 35 minutes until the mixture is pulpy and the onions are completely cooked. Check every now and then and stir. Top up with water if the mixture is too thick before it is fully cooked.

**3** Add the chicken and half the coriander leaves, cover and cook very gently for a few minutes more to cook the chicken through. Mix all the sambal ingredients with the remaining fresh coriander and chilli. Serve the chicken and sambal with the brown rice, heated according to the pack instructions.

PER SERVING 410 kcals, protein 34g, carbs 48g, fat 9g, sat fat 2g, fibre 5g, sugar 15g, salt 1.2g

# Spiced chicken & cauliflower pilaf

*For skin-on chicken breasts why not save money and have a go at jointing a couple of chickens yourself, then freeze the other cuts for the other recipes in this book.*

**TAKES 20 MINUTES ● SERVES 4**

4 chicken breasts, skin on and bone in
1 tbsp medium curry powder (one with turmeric in it)
200g/7oz basmati rice
500ml/18fl oz chicken stock
200g/7oz cauliflower florets
200g/7oz frozen green beans
1 lemon, halved lengthways and sliced
small bunch coriander, leaves and stalks separated and roughly chopped

**1** Heat a frying pan or flameproof casserole and brown the chicken, skin-side down. Tip in the curry powder and rice, fry for 1 minute, then stir in the stock.

**2** Add the cauliflower, beans, lemon slices and coriander stalks to the pan, and turn the chicken skin-side up. Bring to the boil, then simmer with a lid on for 10 minutes, until the chicken is cooked through and the rice is tender. Sprinkle over the coriander leaves and serve.

PER SERVING 360 kcals, protein 41g, carbs 45g, fat 3g, sat fat 1g, fibre 3g, sugar 3g, salt 0.77g

# Thai-spiced chicken patties with noodle salad

*If you wanted to make this easier and even lower in fat you could substitute the chicken for ready minced turkey breast.*

**TAKES 25 MINUTES • SERVES 4**

400g/14oz boneless skinless chicken breast, roughly chopped
1 lemongrass stalk, finely chopped
2 garlic cloves, crushed
zest and juice 1 lime
3 tbsp low-sodium soy sauce
small bunch coriander, chopped
1 red chilli, deseeded and chopped
2 nests medium wheat noodles
300g pack mixed peppers stir-fry vegetables
sweet chilli sauce, to serve (optional)

**1** Heat the grill to medium. Put the chicken in a food processor and pulse until minced. Add the lemongrass, garlic and lime zest with half the soy sauce, coriander and chilli, then pulse again until combined. Tip the mix into a bowl and add some black pepper. Shape into eight patties, then transfer to a non-stick baking sheet and grill for 3–4 minutes each side, until cooked through.

**2** Meanwhile, soak the noodles following the pack instructions, then drain and add the stir-fry vegetables, the remaining soy sauce and the lime juice. Toss well, divide among plates and sprinkle with the remaining coriander and chilli. Serve with the chicken patties and some sweet chilli sauce for dipping, if you like.

PER SERVING 173 kcals, protein 27g, carbs 14g, fat 2g, sat fat none, fibre 2g, sugar 5g, salt 1.48g

# Chargrilled chicken with quinoa tabouleh & tahini dressing

*Fresh, light but still filling, this vibrant recipe would also be great cold as a salad the following day.*

**TAKES 35 MINUTES** ● **SERVES 4**

200g/7oz quinoa
½ cucumber, cut into 1cm/½in chunks
175g/6oz cherry tomatoes, halved
3 spring onions, finely sliced
handful parsley leaves, roughly chopped
handful coriander leaves, roughly chopped
1 tbsp olive oil, plus 1 tsp to griddle
juice 1 lemon
4 boneless skinless chicken breast

**FOR THE TAHINI DRESSING**

1½ tbsp tahini
1½ tbsp low-fat natural yogurt
juice ½ lemon
½ garlic clove, crushed
½ tsp clear honey

**1** Tip the quinoa into a pan and pour over 600ml/1 pint water. Cover with a lid and bring to the boil. Turn down and simmer until the water has evaporated (just as you'd cook rice), about 20 minutes. Take off the lid, set aside and leave to cool.

**2** Tip the cucumber, tomatoes, spring onions and herbs into a large mixing bowl. Pour over the olive oil and lemon juice, season well and mix everything together. Set aside.

**3** Heat a griddle pan and, when smoking hot, rub the chicken with the extra olive oil. Cook for about 5 minutes on each side, depending on its thickness.

**4** Meanwhile, stir together all the dressing ingredients along with 3 tablespoons water. Toss the quinoa together with the salad and arrange on plates. Cut the chicken into thick slices, pile up on the quinoa and drizzle over the dressing.

---

PER SERVING 401 kcals, protein 46g, carbs 31g, fat 11g, sat fat 2g, fibre 1g, sugar 6g, salt 0.24g

# Spiced Singapore noodles with cauliflower, chicken & prawns

*Curry powder is the key ingredient to this low-fat noodle dish; so make sure you use one that's well in date to keep the flavours vibrant.*

**TAKES 45 MINUTES ● SERVES 2**

juice ½ lemon
2 tbsp medium curry powder
300g/10oz cauliflower florets
100g/4oz boneless skinless chicken breast, diced
100g/4oz spring onions, whites and greens separately sliced
200g/7oz white cabbage, cut into chunks
25g/1oz red chilli, deseeded and finely chopped
100g/4oz straight-to-wok fine rice noodles
50g/2oz raw peeled prawns, chopped
1 tbsp soy sauce
½ tsp golden caster sugar
small handful coriander leaves

**1** Heat oven to 180C/160C fan/gas 4. Line a baking sheet with baking parchment. Mix the lemon juice with ½ tablespoon of the curry powder and toss with the cauliflower on the baking sheet. Roast for 25–30 minutes until tender and slightly golden.

**2** Meanwhile, heat a non-stick wok or frying pan and add the chicken, spring-onion whites, cabbage, chilli, remaining curry powder and a splash of water. Fry, adding splashes of water if it starts sticking or looking dry, until the chicken is cooked through and the cabbage is softening. Add the noodles, prawns, soy sauce and sugar, and fry for another few minutes until piping hot and the prawns are cooked.

**3** Scatter over the spring-onion greens, roasted cauliflower and coriander leaves, and serve.

PER SERVING 238 kcals, protein 26g, carbs 25g, fat 3g, sat fat 1g, fibre 10g, sugar 13g, salt 1.7g

# Grilled chicken with chilli & sesame seeds

*You could also dice the chicken and cut the broccoli into pieces to turn this low-fat dish into a stir fry to serve with noodles.*

**TAKES 20 MINUTES** ● **SERVES 2**

2 boneless skinless chicken breasts
1 tbsp vegetable oil
1½ tbsp chilli sauce
2 tsp grated ginger
2 tbsp clear honey
2 tbsp rice vinegar
240g pack Tenderstem broccoli
1 tbsp sesame seeds, toasted

**1** Slice each chicken breast lengthways into two thin pieces. Rub with the oil and season on both sides. Heat a griddle pan and cook the pieces for 2–3 minutes each side.

**2** While the chicken is cooking, mix the chilli sauce, ginger, honey and vinegar with a little seasoning in a small bowl. Brush some of the sauce over the chicken as it cooks – wait until it is grilled on one side first before brushing, or it will burn.

**3** Cook the broccoli in a pan of boiling water for 3–4 minutes until tender. Drain, divide between the plates and pour over all of the remaining sauce. Top with the chicken and sesame seeds.

PER SERVING 303 kcals, protein 35g, carbs 18g, fat 10g, sat fat 2g, fibre 4g, sugar 17g, salt 1g

# One-pan chicken couscous

*As well as being the name for the grain-like balls of semolina, couscous also refers to the Moroccan stew made with it.*

**TAKES 15 MINUTES • SERVES 4**

1 tbsp olive oil

1 onion, thinly sliced

200g/7oz boneless skinless chicken breast, diced

good chunk root ginger

1–2 tbsp harissa paste, plus extra to serve (optional)

10 dried apricots

220g can chickpeas, drained and rinsed

200g/7oz couscous

200ml/7fl oz hot chicken stock

handful coriander leaves, chopped, to garnish

**1** Heat the olive oil in a large frying pan and cook the onion for 1–2 minutes, until softened. Add the chicken and fry for 7–10 minutes until cooked through and the onions have turned golden. Grate over the ginger, stir through the harissa to coat everything and cook for minute more.

**2** Tip in the apricots, chickpeas and couscous, then pour over the stock and stir once. Cover with a lid or tightly cover the pan with foil and leave for about 5 minutes until the couscous has soaked up all the stock and is soft. Fluff up the couscous with a fork and scatter over the coriander to serve. Serve with extra harissa, if you like.

PER SERVING 281 kcals, protein 20g, carbs 41g, fat 6g, sat fat 1g, fibre 3g, sugar 9g, salt 0.48g

# Chicken & lentil stew with gremolata

*Gremolata is a simple mix of lemon, garlic and parsley that gives a finishing flavour lift to everything from a simple stew like this to barbecued lamb and fish.*

**TAKES 1 HOUR • SERVES 4**

2 tbsp olive oil
8 chicken drumsticks, skin on
2 onions, very finely chopped
6 tbsp red split lentils
400g can chopped tomatoes
1 chicken stock cube, crumbled
crusty bread, to serve

**FOR THE GREMOLATA**

zest 1 lemon
1 garlic clove, finely chopped
small handful parsley leaves, finely
  chopped

**1** Heat half the oil in a large flameproof casserole dish, brown the drumsticks on all sides, then transfer to a plate.

**2** Add the onions and remaining oil to the dish, and cook for 5 minutes or so until soft. Add the lentils, tomatoes, 1 can of water and the stock cube. Return the drumsticks to the pan. Bring to the boil, then turn down the heat, put on a lid and simmer for 30 minutes or until tender. Keep an eye on the stew and add a little water if it is drying out. Remove the lid and cook for another 10 minutes, or until the sauce has thickened, then season.

**3** Meanwhile, make the gremolata. Mix the lemon zest, garlic and parsley together. Sprinkle over the cooked stew and serve with a chunk of crusty bread.

PER SERVING 337 kcals, protein 32g, carbs 20g, fat 15g, sat fat 3g, fibre 4g, sugar 7g, salt 1.2g

# Chicken with mushrooms

*Basmati rice, steamed new potatoes or a long flat pasta like tagliatelle would all be nice with this dish and still keep things low in fat.*

**TAKES 40 MINUTES • SERVES 4**

2 tbsp olive oil
500g/1lb 2oz boneless skinless chicken thighs
plain flour, for dusting
50g/2oz cubetti di pancetta
300g/10oz small button mushrooms
2 large shallots, chopped
250ml/9fl oz chicken stock
1 tbsp white wine vinegar
50g/2oz frozen peas
small handful parsley leaves, finely chopped

**1** Heat 1 tablespoon of the oil in a frying pan. Season and dust the chicken with flour, brown on all sides and remove to a plate. Fry the pancetta and mushrooms until softened, then remove.

**2** Add the final tablespoon of oil to the pan and cook the shallots for 5 minutes. Add the stock and vinegar, and bubble for 1–2 minutes. Return the chicken, pancetta and mushrooms to the pan and cook for 15 minutes. Add the peas and parsley, and cook for 2 minutes more, then serve.

PER SERVING 260 kcals, protein 32g, carbs 3g, fat 13g, sat fat 3g, fibre 3g, sugar 1g, salt 0.9g

# Chicken, ginger & green-bean hotpot

*Stringed and sliced runner beans would be just as nice as green beans in this one-pot.*

**TAKES 25 MINUTES • SERVES 2**

½ tbsp vegetable oil

2cm/¾in piece ginger, cut into matchsticks

1 garlic clove, chopped

½ onion, thinly sliced into half moons

1 tbsp Thai fish sauce

½ tbsp soft brown sugar

250g/9oz skinless chicken thigh fillets, trimmed of all fat and cut in half

125ml/4fl oz chicken stock

50g/2oz green beans, trimmed and cut into 2.5cm/1in lengths

1 tbsp chopped coriander leaves

steamed rice, to serve

**1** Heat the oil in a pan over a medium–high heat. Add the ginger, garlic and onion, and stir-fry for about 5 minutes or until lightly golden. Add the fish sauce, sugar, chicken and stock. Cover and cook over a medium heat for 15 minutes.

**2** For the final 3 minutes of cooking, add the green beans. Remove from the heat and stir through half of the coriander. Serve with steamed rice and the remaining coriander scattered over.

PER SERVING 215 kcals, protein 30g, carbs 9g, fat 7g, sat fat 1g, fibre 2g, sugar 7g, salt 2g

# Spicy chicken & bean stew

*A great low-fat one pot to serve to friends – just put it in the middle of the table and let everyone help themselves.*

**TAKES 1½ HOURS** • **SERVES 6**

about 1.25kg/2lb 12oz chicken thighs and drumsticks (we used a 1.2kg mixed pack)
1 tbsp olive oil
2 onions, sliced
1 garlic clove, crushed
2 red chillies, deseeded and chopped
250g/9oz frozen peppers, defrosted
400g can chopped tomatoes
420g can kidney beans in chilli sauce
2 x 400g cans butter beans, drained and rinsed
400ml/14fl oz hot chicken stock
small bunch coriander, chopped
soured cream and crusty bread, to serve

**1** Pull the skin off the chicken and discard. Heat the oil in a large casserole dish, brown the chicken all over, then remove to a plate with a slotted spoon. Tip in the onions, garlic and chillies, then fry for 5 minutes until starting to soften and turn golden.

**2** Add the peppers, tomatoes, beans and hot stock. Put the chicken back on top, half-cover with a pan lid and cook for 50 minutes, until the chicken is cooked through and tender. Stir through the coriander and serve with soured cream and crusty bread.

PER SERVING 366 kcals, protein 38g, carbs 30g, fat 11g, sat fat 5g, fibre 9g, sugar 12g, salt 2.45g

# Chicken, chickpea & lemon casserole

*This lightly spiced one-pot can be easily halved for a solo supper or just as easily doubled for four.*

**TAKES 40 MINUTES ● SERVES 2**

175g/6oz new potatoes, halved

1 medium onion, thinly sliced

2 slices lemon, chopped

2 garlic cloves, roughly chopped

1 tsp ground cumin

1 tsp ground cinnamon

450ml/16fl oz chicken stock

2 large skinless boneless chicken thighs, trimmed of all fat and cut into cubes

½ x 410g can chickpeas, drained and rinsed

handful coriander leaves, chopped

steamed green beans or broccoli, to serve

**1** Put the potatoes, onion, lemon and garlic into a casserole or heavy pan. Sprinkle over the ground spices and season lightly. Toss together then pour over the stock. Bring to the boil and simmer for 12 minutes or until the potatoes are tender.

**2** Add the chicken and chickpeas, cover the pan and simmer gently for a further 10–12 minutes or until the chicken is cooked through. Check the seasoning and stir in the coriander. Serve with steamed green beans or broccoli.

PER SERVING 310 kcals, protein 34g, carbs 32g, fat 6g, sat fat 1g, fibre 4g, sugar none, salt 1.4g

# All-in-one chicken, squash & new-potato casserole

*This superhealthy supper is a great option for those trying to lower their cholesterol intake.*

**TAKES 45 MINUTES • SERVES 2**

¼ small butternut squash, peeled and diced (about 200g/7oz total)

8 small new potatoes

1 tsp ground coriander

1 tbsp thyme leaves

600ml/1 pint chicken stock

1 garlic clove, crushed

2 skinless chicken breasts

175g/6oz prepared French beans, courgette or broccoli

25g/1oz pitted green olives in brine, drained

**1** Heat oven to 190C/170C fan/gas 5. Put the butternut squash, potatoes, ground coriander, thyme, stock and garlic into a flameproof casserole. Season and bring to the boil, then simmer gently for 10 minutes.

**2** Tuck in the chicken breasts, making sure that they are submerged. Cover and transfer to the oven for 15 minutes until the chicken is cooked through. Lift out the chicken and veg, set aside and keep warm, then boil the stock until reduced by half. Add the green veg and olives and simmer until cooked. Season and serve.

PER SERVING 413 kcals, protein 41g, carbs 50g, fat 7g, sat fat 2g, fibre 8g, sugar 13g, salt 1g

# Moroccan chicken with courgettes

*Use the flavour base to this casserole as a blueprint and add diced aubergine, red-pepper chunks or slices of carrot as well as the courgette.*

**TAKES 30 MINUTES ● SERVES 4**

4 skinless chicken breasts
1 tsp ground cumin
1 tbsp olive oil
1 onion, finely sliced
400g can cherry tomatoes
2 tbsp harissa paste
1 tbsp clear honey
2 medium courgettes, thickly sliced
400g can chickpeas, drained and rinsed

**1** Season the chicken breasts all over with the cumin and lots of ground black pepper. Heat the oil in a large non-stick frying pan and cook the chicken with the onions for 4 minutes. Turn the chicken over and cook for a further 3 minutes. Stir the onions around the chicken regularly as they cook.

**2** Tip the tomatoes and 250ml/9fl oz water into the pan and stir in the harissa, honey, courgettes and chickpeas. Bring to a gentle simmer and cook for 15 minutes until the chicken is tender and the sauce has thickened slightly.

PER SERVING 293 kcals, protein 36g, carbs 22g, fat 6g, sat fat 1g, fibre 4g, sugar 10g, salt 0.9g

# One-pot lentil chicken

*If you wanted to make this healthy stew for two even easier, swap the lentils for a pouch of ready cooked ones and just add them at the end.*

**TAKES 40 MINUTES • SERVES 2**

1 tsp vegetable oil

2 rashers lean dry-cure back bacon, trimmed and chopped

2 large bone-in chicken thighs, skin removed

1 medium onion, thinly sliced

1 garlic clove, thinly sliced

2 tsp plain flour

2 tsp tomato purée

150ml/¼ pint dry white wine

200ml/7fl oz chicken stock

50g/2oz green lentils

½ tsp dried thyme

85g/3oz chestnut mushrooms, halved if large

**1** Heat the oil in a wide, shallow non-stick pan, add the bacon and fry briskly until lightly coloured, then lift on to a plate. Add the chicken and fry on each side until lightly brown. Set aside with the bacon.

**2** Tip the onion and garlic into the pan and cook for 5 minutes. Stir in the flour and tomato purée, then stir over a low heat for 2–3 minutes. Add the wine, stock, lentils and thyme. Bring to the boil, reduce the heat, then cover and simmer for 5 minutes.

**3** Stir in the mushrooms. Add the bacon and chicken, pushing them under the liquid. Cover and simmer for 20–25 minutes, or until the lentils are tender and the chicken cooked. Season with salt and pepper to taste and serve.

PER SERVING 360 kcals, protein 41g, carbs 14g, fat 10g, sat fat 3g, fibre 6g, sugar none, salt 2.4g

# Squash, chicken & couscous one-pot

*Couscous is often cooked and served separately, but here it's cleverly cooked with everything else so that it absorbs all the flavours of the other ingredients.*

**TAKES 1 HOUR ● SERVES 4**

2 tbsp harissa paste
1 tsp each ground cumin and ground coriander
2 red onions, halved and cut into thin wedges
2 boneless skinless chicken breasts, cut into bite-size chunks
1 small butternut squash, cut into 1cm/½in chunks (no need to peel)
2 x 400g cans tomatoes
zest and juice 2 lemons
200g/7oz cherry tomatoes, halved
140g/5oz couscous
small bunch coriander, roughly chopped

**1** Heat a large non-stick casserole dish or pan on the hob. Add the harissa, spices and onions, then stir and cook gently for 10 minutes until soft. Add the chicken and brown for 5–10 minutes. Add the squash, stirring to combine, and a splash of water if it starts to stick. Cook for 5 minutes more.

**2** Tip the canned tomatoes into the pan with a can of water, then cover and simmer for 20–30 minutes. Add the lemon zest and juice, cherry tomatoes, couscous and some seasoning. Cover and turn off the heat. Leave on the hob for 10 minutes, then stir through the coriander and serve.

PER SERVING 283 kcals, protein 25g, carbs 42g, fat 3g, sat fat 1g, fibre 6g, sugar 16g, salt 0.53g

# Easy chicken tagine

*If you can't find dried cherries for this Moroccan stew, dried apricots or cranberries would be just as nice.*

**TAKES 1 HOUR • SERVES 6**

2 onions, 1 roughly chopped, 1 sliced
100g/4oz tomatoes
100g/4oz ginger, roughly chopped
3 garlic cloves
4 boneless skinless chicken breasts
3 tbsp olive oil
1 tsp turmeric powder
1 tbsp each ground cumin, coriander
    and cinnamon
1 large butternut squash, deseeded
    and cut into big chunks
600ml/1 pint chicken stock
2 tbsp brown sugar
2 tbsp red wine vinegar
100g/4oz dried cherries

**TO GARNISH**

1 small red onion, finely chopped
zest 1 lemon
handful mint leaves
100g/4oz feta, crumbled
couscous and natural yogurt, to serve

**1** Whizz the chopped onion, tomatoes, ginger and garlic into a rough paste in a food processor and set aside. Season the chicken. Heat 2 tablespoons of the oil in a flameproof dish, then brown the chicken on all sides. Remove the chicken to a plate. Fry the sliced onion in the remaining oil in the dish until softened, then add the spices and fry for 1 minute more until fragrant. Add the onion paste and fry for another few minutes to soften.
**2** Return the chicken to the dish with the squash, stock, sugar and vinegar. Bring to a simmer, then cook for 30 minutes until the chicken is cooked through. Lift the chicken out and stir in the cherries, then continue simmering the sauce to thicken while you shred the chicken into bite-size chunks. Stir the chicken back into the sauce and season.
**3** Combine the red onion, lemon zest, mint and feta. Scatter over the dish, then serve with some couscous and yogurt.

PER SERVING 324 kcals, protein 27g, carbs 39g, fat 7g, sat fat 1g, fibre 6g, sugar 24g, salt 0.4g

# Chicken & pomegranate bulghar pilaf

*Pomegranate is packed with vitamin C, and using the seeds in a dish is like adding little juice bombs that burst with flavour when you bite into them.*

**TAKES 45 MINUTES • SERVES 4**

sunflower oil, for frying

8 chicken thigh fillets, skin removed, each cut into 2–3 pieces

2 tbsp ras el hanout or Moroccan spice mix

500ml/18fl oz hot chicken stock

350g/12oz bulghar wheat

bunch mint, most chopped, reserving a few leaves

2 x 100g tubs pomegranate seeds

**1** Heat a little oil in a large casserole dish (with a tight-fitting lid). Coat the chicken pieces with some seasoning and half of the spice mix, and add to the dish. Brown well on all sides.

**2** Add the remaining spice mix and cook for 1 minute. Pour over the stock, season and stir, then cover and cook for 25 minutes over a low–medium heat.

**3** Remove the lid, increase the heat to a medium simmer and add the bulghar wheat. Cook for 10 minutes, then re-cover, turn off the heat and leave to stand for a further 10 minutes.

**4** When all the liquid has been absorbed and the bulghar wheat is tender, stir through the chopped mint and scatter over the pomegranate seeds and add extra mint leaves.

PER SERVING 488 kcals, protein 32g, carbs 71g, fat 8g, sat fat 1g, fibre 1g, sugar 8g, salt 0.5g

# Spicy chicken couscous

*If you like fried-rice dishes then you'll love this much healthier recipe. Any leftovers can be packed into a lunchbox the next day.*

**TAKES 30 MINUTES ● SERVES 4**

250g/9oz couscous
3 tbsp olive oil
1 chopped onion
2 large skinless chicken breast fillets, sliced
85g/3oz blanched almonds
1 tbsp hot curry paste
100g/4oz halved ready-to-eat apricots
small pack coriander
natural yogurt, to serve (optional)

**1** Prepare the couscous according to the pack instructions. Heat the olive oil in a pan and cook the onion for 2–3 minutes until softened.

**2** Toss in the chicken breast fillets and stir-fry for 5–6 minutes until tender. Add the blanched almonds and, when golden, stir in the hot curry paste and cook for 1 minute more.

**3** Add the couscous to the pan along with the apricots and the coriander. Toss until hot then serve with natural yogurt, if you like.

PER SERVING 424 kcals, protein 18g, carbs 46g, fat 20g, sat fat 5g, fibre 3g, sugar none, salt 1.69g

# Chicken & sweet-potato curry

*This recipe unashamedly makes use of a jar of curry paste, which is a huge time-saver when you are after a quick weeknight supper that doesn't compromise on flavour.*

**TAKES 55 MINUTES • SERVES 4**

1 tsp sunflower oil
1 onion, chopped
450g/1lb boneless skinless chicken
   breast, cut into bite-size pieces
165g jar korma paste
2 garlic cloves, crushed
500g/1lb 2oz sweet potatoes, cut into
   small chunks
400g can chopped tomatoes
100g bag baby leaf spinach
cooked basmati rice, to serve

**1** Heat the oil in a pan, add the onion and cook over a low heat for about 5 minutes until softened. Increase the heat slightly, add the chicken pieces and brown.

**2** Stir in the curry paste and garlic, cooking for 2 minutes before adding 100ml/3½fl oz water, the sweet potatoes and chopped tomatoes. Simmer for 20–30 minutes until the chicken is cooked through and the sweet potatoes are tender – add a splash more water if it starts to look dry. Season to taste and add the spinach, removing the pan from the heat and stirring until the spinach has wilted. Serve with cooked basmati rice.

PER SERVING 365 kcals, protein 32g, carbs 36g, fat 10g, sat fat 3g, fibre 7g, sugar 15g, salt 1.8g

# Harissa-spiced chicken with bulghar wheat

*If you can't find harissa paste then a good substitute is the same amount of tomato purée mixed with a healthy pinch of chilli powder.*

**TAKES 30 MINUTES • SERVES 4**

1 tbsp harissa paste
4 skinless chicken breasts
1 tbsp vegetable or sunflower oil
1 onion, halved and sliced
2 tbsp pine nuts
handful ready-to-eat dried apricots
300g/10oz bulghar wheat
600ml/1 pint hot chicken stock (from a cube)
handful coriander, leaves only, chopped

**1** Rub the harissa paste over the chicken. Heat the oil in a deep non-stick pan, then fry the chicken for about 3 minutes on each side, until just golden (it won't be cooked through at this stage). Remove and set aside.

**2** Add the onion, then gently fry for 5 minutes until soft. Tip in the pine nuts and continue cooking for another few minutes until toasted. Tip in the apricots, bulghar and stock, then season and cover. Cook for about 10 minutes until the stock is almost absorbed.

**3** Return the chicken to the pan, re-cover and cook for 5 minutes on a low heat until the liquid has been absorbed and the chicken is cooked through. Fluff up the bulghar with a fork and scatter with the coriander to serve.

PER SERVING 536 kcals, protein 49g, carbs 65g, fat 11g, sat fat 2g, fibre 2g, sugar 8g, salt 1.06g

# Easy one-pot chicken casserole

*Turn this dish into a celebration of spring by using whole baby carrots instead of batons.*

**TAKES 55 MINUTES • SERVES 4**

8 bone-in chicken thighs, skin pulled off
 and discarded
1 tbsp oil
5 spring onions, sliced, white and green
 parts kept separate
2 tbsp plain flour
2 chicken stock cubes
2 large carrots, cut into batons
400g/14oz new potatoes, halved
 if large
200g/7oz frozen peas
1 tbsp grainy mustard
small handful soft herbs, like parsley,
 chives, dill or tarragon, chopped

**1** Fry the thighs in the oil in a flameproof casserole dish or wide pan with a lid to brown. Stir in the whites of the spring onions with the flour, crumble in the stock cubes and stir for a minute or 2.

**2** Gradually stir in 750ml/1¼ pints hot water from the kettle. Throw in the carrots and potatoes, and bring to a simmer. Cover and cook for 20 minutes.

**3** Take off the lid and simmer for 15 minutes more, then throw in the peas for another 5 minutes. Season, stir in the mustard, green spring-onion bits, herbs and some seasoning.

PER SERVING 386 kcals, protein 43g, carbs 33g, fat 10g, sat fat 2g, fibre 6g, sugar 8g, salt 2.1g

# Spring chicken in a pot

*As well as being the easiest of pasta sauces, pesto can also be added to stews and gravies.*

**TAKES 1 HOUR ● SERVES 4**

1 tbsp olive oil
1 onion, chopped
500g/1lb 2oz boneless skinless chicken
   thighs
300g/10oz small new potatoes
300ml/½ pint low-salt vegetable stock
   (such as Kallo low-salt vegetable
   stock cubes)
350g/12oz broccoli, cut into small
   florets
350g/12oz spring greens, shredded
140g/5oz petits pois
bunch spring onions, sliced
2 tbsp green pesto sauce

**1** Heat the oil in a large, heavy pan. Add the onion, gently fry for 5 minutes until softened, add the chicken, then fry until lightly coloured. Add the potatoes, stock and plenty of freshly ground black pepper, then bring to the boil. Cover, then simmer for 30 minutes until the potatoes are tender and the chicken is cooked. Can be frozen at this point.
**2** Add the broccoli, spring greens, petits pois and spring onions, stir well, then return to the boil. Cover, then cook for 5 minutes more, then stir in the pesto and heat through.

PER SERVING 339 kcals, protein 36g, carbs 27g, fat 10g, sat fat 3g, fibre 8g, sugar 12g, salt 0.5g

# Teriyaki-chicken meatballs with rice & greens

*If you wanted to cheat a little with this recipe, swap the mirin, soy and sugar for 100ml/3½fl oz ready-made teriyaki sauce.*

**TAKES 25 MINUTES • SERVES 4**

2 shallots
1 carrot, cut into chunks
500g/1lb 2oz boneless skinless chicken
    breasts or thighs, cut into chunks
zest and juice 1 lemon
a little oil
200g/7oz basmati rice
200g/7oz spring greens, chopped
100ml/3½fl oz mirin
3 tbsp soy sauce
3 tbsp caster sugar

**1** Heat oven to 200C/180C fan/gas 6. Pulse the shallots and carrot in a food processor until finely chopped. Add the chicken, lemon zest and some seasoning, and pulse again until mixed. Using oiled hands, shape into small meatballs. Put on a baking sheet lined with baking parchment and bake for 10 minutes until browned and cooked through.
**2** Meanwhile, boil the rice according to the pack instructions, adding the spring greens for the final 4 minutes. Drain well.
**3** Add the mirin, soy, lemon juice and sugar to a pan. Bring to the boil, then simmer until saucy. Remove from the heat, add the meatballs to the pan and roll them around in the sauce. Divide the rice and greens among plates or bowls and spoon the meatballs over.

PER SERVING 481 kcals, protein 36g, carbs 70g, fat 2g, sat fat 1g, fibre 3g, sugar 28g, salt 2.3g

# Cook-with-kids fajitas

*A great recipe to either make with kids or let them assemble themselves at the table and still feel like they've helped.*

**TAKES 35 MINUTES, PLUS MARINATING ● SERVES 4**

4 boneless skinless chicken breasts, cut into chunks

4 limes, juice only

2 tsp fajita seasoning

olive oil, for frying

grated cheese, soured cream and 6–8 tortillas, to serve

**FOR THE SALSA**

1 red pepper

4 ripe tomatoes

small bunch coriander, leaves picked

½ lime, juice only

**FOR THE GUACAMOLE**

2 very ripe avocados, halved and stone removed

½ lime, juice only

**1** In a bowl coat the chicken in the lime juice and seasoning, cover, then leave to marinate in the fridge for at least 2 hours.

**2** Roughly chop the pepper and tomatoes for the salsa. Younger children can pick the leaves from the coriander. Tip all the salsa ingredients into a food processor and pulse until finely chopped. Set aside.

**3** For the guacamole, squeeze or spoon the avocado into a bowl and use a potato masher to mash it. Stir in the lime juice and some black pepper with a spoon.

**4** Heat a little olive oil in a frying pan and tip in the chicken. Cook for 5–8 minutes or until the chicken chunks are cooked through. Put the grated cheese, salsa, guacamole and soured cream in separate colourful bowls to put on the table. Heat the tortillas according to the pack instructions and put the cooked chicken in a bowl. Show children how to fill and roll their tortilla.

PER SERVING 267 kcals, protein 32g, carbs 7g, fat 12g, sat fat 3g, fibre 4g, sugar 5g, salt 0.8g

# All-in-one roast chicken & veg

*Sometimes you're just cooking for two and don't want to go to the effort of making a big roast, in which case here's an easy solution.*

**TAKES 1 HOUR ● SERVES 2**

8 baby new potatoes, halved
2 tsp olive oil
2 carrots, sliced
1 courgette, sliced
1 leek, sliced
1 tsp each chopped thyme and
    rosemary, plus a sprig or two
2 small skinless chicken breasts
150ml/¼ pint low-sodium chicken
    stock

**1** Heat oven to 200C/180C fan/gas 6. Toss the potatoes in a small roasting tin with the oil, carrots, courgette, leek, herbs and some seasoning.

**2** Roast for 30 minutes until starting to brown. Remove from the oven and give the veg a stir, nestle in the chicken, then return to the oven for 15 minutes. Pour over the stock, then cook for 5 minutes more or until the chicken and veg are cooked through and you have a tasty gravy.

PER SERVING 300 kcals, protein 34g, carbs 27g, fat 7g, sat fat 1g, fibre 5g, sugar 10g, salt 0.32g

# Chicken & leek pot pies

*Here we've combined the flavour of a chicken pie and the mash topping of a shepherd's pie and still managed to keep it low fat.*

**TAKES 1 HOUR 10 MINUTES**
● **SERVES 4**

500g/1lb 2oz parsnips, peeled
300g/10oz floury potatoes, peeled
500g/1lb 2oz boneless skinless chicken
   breasts
2 tsp cornflour
1 tbsp olive oil
4 leeks, sliced
grated zest 1 lemon
2 tbsp chopped parsley
2 tbsp low-fat crème fraîche
1 tbsp wholegrain mustard

**1** Heat oven to 200C/180C fan/gas 6. Chop the parsnips and potatoes into chunks, then boil for 15 minutes until tender. Drain, reserving the water, then mash with a little seasoning.

**2** Cut the chicken into small chunks, then toss in the cornflour. Heat the oil in a large pan, add the leeks, then fry for 3 minutes until starting to soften. Add the chicken and 200ml/7fl oz water from the potatoes, then bring to the boil, stirring. Reduce the heat, then gently simmer for 10 minutes, until the chicken is just tender. Remove from the heat, then stir in the lemon zest, parsley, crème fraîche and mustard.

**3** Divide the chicken filling among four 300ml pie dishes. Spoon over the mash and spread roughly with a fork to seal in the filling. Bake for 25 minutes until the topping is crisp and golden.

PER SERVING 486 kcals, protein 28g, carbs 45g, fat 23g, sat fat 2g, fibre 9g, none, salt 0.56g

# Jerk-chicken burger

*Roasted sweet-potato fries would make the perfect side dish to serve with these guilt-free burgers.*

**TAKES 20 MINUTES • SERVES 2**

2 boneless skinless chicken breasts
few thyme sprigs, leaves picked
1 tbsp olive oil
2 tsp jerk seasoning
juice 1 lime
2 large bread rolls, cut in half
½ small mango, stoned, peeled and
    sliced
1 tomato, sliced
1 Little Gem lettuce heart, shredded
2 tbsp mayonnaise and tomato
    ketchup, to garnish each burger
    (optional)

**1** Put the chicken breasts between pieces of cling film and bash with a rolling pin to flatten. Mix together the thyme, oil, jerk seasoning and half the lime juice in a bowl. Add the chicken and leave to marinate for 5 minutes.

**2** Heat a griddle pan until hot and cook the chicken for 4–5 minutes each side or until cooked through. Remove from the heat. Meanwhile, toast the cut sides of the buns for 1–2 minutes.

**3** Put the chicken on the buns and top with the mango, tomato and a handful of lettuce. Squeeze over the rest of the lime and top with mayo and ketchup, if you like.

PER SERVING 417 kcals, protein 38g, carbs 45g, fat 9g, sat fat 2g, fibre 4g, sugar 11g, salt 1.2g

# Tagliatelle with grilled chicken & tomatoes

*Whether or not you serve with Parmesan just depends on how low fat you want to make this easy pasta dish.*

**TAKES 25 MINUTES • SERVES 4**

4 boneless skinless chicken breasts
zest and juice 1 lemon
1 tbsp chopped tarragon leaves or
  1 tsp dried
2 tsp olive oil
8 small tomatoes, halved
300g/10oz tagliatelle

**1** Heat the grill to high. Coat the chicken with the lemon zest and juice, tarragon and some salt and pepper. Put in a large, shallow ovenproof dish or roasting tin in one layer. Brush lightly with a little of the oil, then grill for 6 minutes. Turn the chicken over and add the tomatoes to the dish or tin, cut-side up, brushing them lightly with more of the oil. Grill for a further 6–8 minutes until the chicken is cooked and lightly browned and the tomatoes are tender.

**2** Meanwhile, cook the pasta in a large pan of boiling water according to the pack instructions. Drain well, reserving 150ml/¼ pint of the cooking water, then return to the pan. Remove the chicken from the dish or tin and cut into chunks. Add to the pasta with the tomatoes, cooking water and pan juices. Toss everything together well and serve.

PER SERVING 423 kcals, protein 40g, carbs 61g, fat 4g, sat fat 1g, fibre 3g, sugar 4g, salt 0.48g

# Cajun meatballs

*As the meatballs are made with pure minced chicken, their texture is quite firm. You can make softer ones by adding 25g/1oz fresh breadcrumbs.*

**TAKES 40 MINUTES • SERVES 4**

2 tbsp each butter and plain flour
1 onion, finely chopped
1 green pepper, deseeded and finely
    chopped
2 celery sticks, finely chopped
2 garlic cloves, chopped
1 bay leaf
400g can plum tomatoes
1 chicken stock cube
dash Tabasco or hot pepper sauce
4 spring onions, finely sliced
handful coriander leaves, roughly
    chopped
cooked rice or mash, to serve

**FOR THE MEATBALLS**

1 tbsp Cajun spice mix
500g pack minced chicken or turkey
1 tbsp vegetable oil

**1** Put the butter in a pan over a low heat. Stir in the flour and cook, stirring all the time to make a paste. Cook until the paste is hazelnut brown in colour – make sure that it doesn't burn. Tip in the vegetables, garlic and bay leaf, stir briefly, then pour in the tomatoes and 1½ cans water. Crumble in the stock cube, add the hot sauce, then cover and cook for 15 minutes, stirring occasionally, while you make the meatballs.
**2** Work the spice and some seasoning into the mince. Try not to over-handle or it will toughen. Shape into 20 meatballs.
**3** Heat the oil in a large non-stick pan and quickly brown the meatballs in batches until they are nicely coloured on all sides.
**4** Stir the sauce, then drop in the meatballs and cook on a low heat for 10 minutes until the meatballs are cooked through. Scatter over the spring onions and coriander, and serve with rice or mash.

PER SERVING 299 kcals, protein 34g, carbs 16g, fat 11g, sat fat 5g, fibre 3g, sugar 7g, salt 1.2g

# Tortilla pie

*Using corn tortillas is a clever way of including a delicious topping without adding the calories that using pastry would bring.*

**TAKES 30 MINUTES ● SERVES 7**

2 onions, finely chopped
1 tbsp olive oil, plus a little extra if
  needed
2 tsp ground cumin
500g/1lb 2oz minced chicken or turkey
1½ tbsp chipotle paste
400g can chopped tomatoes
400g can kidney beans, drained and
  rinsed
198g can sweetcorn, drained
2 corn tortillas, snipped into triangles
small handful grated Cheddar
2 spring onions, finely sliced

**1** In a deep, flameproof casserole dish, cook the onions in the oil for 8 minutes until soft. Add the cumin and cook for 1 minute more. Stir in the mince and add a bit more oil, if needed. Turn up the heat and cook for 4–6 minutes, stirring occasionally, until the mince is browned.
**2** Stir in the chipotle paste, tomatoes and half a can of water, and simmer for 5 minutes. Mix in the beans and sweetcorn, and cook for a few minutes more until thick, piping hot and the mince is cooked.
**3** Heat the grill. Take the pan off the heat and put the tortilla triangles randomly on top. Scatter over the cheese and grill for a few minutes until the topping is crisp, taking care that it doesn't burn. Sprinkle with the spring onions and serve.

PER SERVING 210 kcals, protein 24g, carbs 14g, fat 6g, sat fat 2g, fibre 4g, sugar 6g, salt 1.5g

# Pick & mix noodle plate

*A great recipe for fussy eaters as they can pick and choose what they want – but at least you can rest assured that all kids love crumbed chicken.*

**TAKES 35 MINUTES ● SERVES 4**

2 skinless chicken breasts, cut into
    finger-length strips
1 egg, beaten
50g/2oz breadcrumbs
200g/7oz medium egg noodles
2 tbsp olive oil
4 spring onions, chopped
½ cucumber
1 large carrot
hoisin, plum or barbecue sauce, for
    dipping

**1** Heat oven to 200C/180C fan/gas 6. Dip the chicken strips into the beaten egg, shake off the excess, then roll in breadcrumbs to coat. Put on a non-stick baking sheet and bake for 15–20 minutes or until crisp and cooked through.
**2** Meanwhile, cook the noodles according to the pack instructions. Drain and toss with the olive oil and spring onions. Using a vegetable peeler, shave the cucumber and the carrot into ribbons. Pile the noodles on to serving plates along with the carrot and cucumber. Put a few chicken strips alongside, and serve with a little pot of hoisin, plum or barbecue sauce for dipping.

PER SERVING (NO SAUCE) 388 kcals, protein 24g, carbs 50g, fat 12g, sat fat 2g, fibre 3g, sugar 6g, salt 0.63g

# Chicken & coriander burgers with guacamole

*In recipes like this chicken and turkey mince are completely interchangeable; so use whichever is easier to find.*

**TAKES 30 MINUTES ● SERVES 4**

400g/14oz minced chicken or turkey

1 tsp Worcestershire sauce

85g/3oz fresh breadcrumbs

1 tbsp chopped coriander leaves

1 red onion, finely chopped

2 small ripe avocados or 1 large

1 red chilli, deseeded and finely chopped

juice 1 lime

4 ciabatta rolls, cut in half

1 tsp sunflower oil

8 red peppers, roughly chopped

**1** Mix the mince, Worcestershire sauce, breadcrumbs, half each of the coriander and onion and some seasoning until combined. Form into four burgers, then chill until ready to cook.

**2** To make the guacamole, mash the avocado with the remaining coriander and onion, the chilli and lime juice, and season.

**3** Heat a griddle pan or barbecue until hot. Griddle the rolls, cut-side down, for 1 minute, then keep warm. Brush the burgers with the oil to keep them from sticking. Cook for 7–8 minutes on each side until charred and cooked through. Fill the rolls with the burgers, guacamole and peppers.

PER SERVING 467 kcals, protein 35g, carbs 51g, fat 14g, sat fat 3g, fibre 6g, sugar 6g, salt 1.4g

# Spicy chicken & pepper bake

*Prepare this cheap and healthy family meal ahead and freeze – to cook from frozen add about 40 minutes on to the baking time.*

**TAKES 1 HOUR** ● **SERVES 4**

1kg/2lb 4oz potatoes, chopped
25g/1oz butter
300g/10oz frozen peppers
1 onion, chopped
500g/1lb 2oz minced chicken or turkey
1 red chilli, deseeded and chopped
1 tbsp smoked paprika
200ml/7fl oz hot chicken stock

**1** Heat oven to 200C/180C fan/gas 6. Cook the potatoes in a large pan of salted water for 12–15 minutes or until tender. Drain well, then return to the pan and allow to steam for 3 minutes. Add some seasoning and the butter, then roughly mash with a fork and set aside until later.

**2** Meanwhile, cook the peppers and onion in a large pan for 5 minutes – the water in the peppers should stop them sticking. Stir in the chicken mince, chilli and paprika, and cook until browned. Pour in the stock, then bubble for 10 minutes until thickened. Transfer the mince into an ovenproof dish, top with the mash and cook for 30 minutes or until golden and bubbling.

---

PER SERVING 409 kcals, protein 38g, carbs 47g, fat 8g, sat fat 4g, fibre 6g, sugar 6g, salt 0.5g

# Piri-piri chicken with spicy rice

*Kids love the flavour of piri-piri chicken – just choose a spice level for the marinade that suits their chilli tolerance.*

**TAKES 1 HOUR ● SERVES 4**

about 4 skin-on chicken thighs and 4 drumsticks
6 tbsp piri-piri marinade (you can buy mild, medium or hot)
1 tbsp sunflower oil
2 peppers, any colour, deseeded and finely chopped
½ bunch spring onions, sliced, white and green parts separated
4 tbsp tomato purée
1 tbsp sweet smoked paprika
300g/10oz cooked rice
favourite vegetables and salad, to serve (optional)

**1** Heat oven to 200C/180C fan/gas 6. Slash each piece of chicken three times, so the marinade can really flavour the meat. Pour over the piri-piri sauce and leave in the fridge to marinate, if you have time. If not, mix well and arrange, skin-side up, in a roasting tin. Cook for 30 minutes, then increase heat to 220C/200C fan/gas 7 and cook for about 15 minutes more until the skin is crispy and golden.

**2** When the chicken is almost ready, heat the oil in a frying pan. Cook the peppers and white parts of the spring onions for 5 minutes. Tip in the purée and paprika, stir, then add the rice, breaking it up with a wooden spoon so all the grains are coated well. Turn up to a high heat and scrape any bits that are stuck on the bottom of the pan so you get some soft and some crispy parts. Heat until piping hot. Serve the chicken and rice, scattered with the green parts of the spring onion, with some vegetables or salad, if you like.

PER SERVING 606 kcals, protein 35g, carbs 56g, fat 25g, sat fat 5g, fibre 3g, sugar 8g, salt 1.2g

# Herbed meatballs

*Mix and match the herbs in this dish to suit what you have available – thyme, rosemary, basil, coriander and tarragon would all work well.*

**TAKES 30 MINUTES ● SERVES 5**

85g/3oz breadcrumbs
75ml/2½fl oz milk
350g/12oz minced chicken or turkey
2 tsp dried oregano
small bunch flat-leaf parsley, chopped
2 tsp olive oil
680g jar onion and garlic passata
4 tsp sugar
500g bag pasta shapes

**1** Tip the crumbs into a large bowl, then stir in the milk until the crumbs have absorbed the liquid. Add the mince, 1 teaspoon of the oregano and half the parsley, then season and mix with a fork. Use wet hands to shape into 30 meatballs.

**2** Heat the oil in a large non-stick pan, then brown the meatballs for 5 minutes, turning to cook all over. Pour in the passata, sugar, remaining oregano and most of the remaining parsley. Stir well, then simmer for 8–10 minutes until the meatballs are just cooked through.

**3** Meanwhile, cook the pasta according to the pack instructions. Season the sauce, spoon the meatballs and sauce over the pasta, then sprinkle over any remaining parsley to serve.

PER SERVING 260 kcals, protein 25g, carbs 33g, fat 4g, sat fat 1g, fibre 1g, sugar 12g, salt 1.45g

# Chicken & sweetcorn egg-fried rice

*A great way of stretching another family meal out of some leftover cooked rice and chicken.*

**TAKES 15 MINUTES • SERVES 4**

1 tbsp sunflower oil
3 eggs, beaten with some seasoning
320g pack mixed stir-fry veg
1 tbsp mild curry powder
140g/5oz frozen sweetcorn
600g/1lb 5oz cooked rice
1 roasted chicken breast, finely
    shredded
2 tbsp low-salt soy sauce
2 tbsp sweet chilli sauce
2 tbsp tomato ketchup

**1** Heat a splash of the oil in a large frying pan and tip in the beaten eggs. Swirl the pan to coat in a thin layer of egg and cook for a few minutes until set. Tip on to a chopping board, roll up, slice thinly and set aside.

**2** Heat a little more of the oil, add the stir-fry veg, curry powder and sweetcorn with a splash of water. Cook for 1–2 minutes until the veg starts to wilt, then tip into a bowl. Add the last of the oil to the pan, tip in the rice and chicken, mix well, then add the soy sauce, sweet chilli, ketchup, a splash of water and some black pepper.

**3** Finally, add the eggs and the veg to the pan, toss everything together and heat through until hot. Tip into bowls and serve immediately.

PER SERVING 443 kcals, protein 23g, carbs 60g, fat 11g, sat fat 2g, fibre 4g, sugar 10g, salt 1.6g

# Italian chicken bake

*This may not be low-fat but a single serving provides two of your five-a-day vegetable count.*

**TAKES 1 HOUR • SERVES 4**

2 small onions or 1 large, chopped
2 garlic cloves, crushed
3 tbsp olive oil
2 tsp dried oregano
3 x 400g cans chopped tomatoes or cherry tomatoes
1 tbsp sugar
little splash red or white wine vinegar
about 500g/1lb 2oz cooked chicken, shredded into chunks
125g ball mozzarella
2 good handfuls fresh breadcrumbs

**1** Fry the onion and garlic in the oil until softened. Add the oregano, tomatoes and sugar, a little splash of vinegar and some seasoning, then simmer for 20 minutes until really thick. Stir in the chicken and transfer to a baking dish.
**2** Heat oven to 220C/200C fan/gas 7. Tear over the mozzarella in chunks, then scatter over the breadcrumbs with a bit more ground black pepper. Bake for 20 minutes until the chicken is piping hot throughout and the top is golden and bubbling.

PER SERVING 475 kcals, protein 44g, carbs 21g, fat 25g, sat fat 8g, fibre 4g, sugar 16g, salt 0.9g

# Caesar chicken burgers

*If you can't find minced chicken you can very finely chop chicken breasts by hand or pulse in a food processor.*

**TAKES 35 MINUTES ● SERVES 4**

1 garlic clove, crushed
1 anchovy, diced (optional)
juice 1 lemon
3 tbsp grated Parmesan
small bunch parsley, finely chopped
3 tbsp low-fat Greek-style yogurt
500g/1lb 2oz minced chicken or turkey
1 onion, finely chopped
1 romaine lettuce, shredded
4 small wholemeal buns, cut in half
2 tomatoes, sliced

**1** Heat oven to 200C/180C fan/gas 6. Mix together the garlic, anchovy (if using), lemon juice, two-thirds of the Parmesan and the parsley. Put half in a small bowl, mix with the yogurt and set aside. Mix the other half in a large bowl with the mince and onion, then season. Shape into four burgers and put in a roasting tin, then cook for 15–20 minutes, until cooked through.
**2** Meanwhile, mix the lettuce with the yogurt dressing and slice the buns. To assemble, put the burgers in the buns with some of the lettuce salad and a few tomato slices. Serve the burgers with the remaining salad sprinkled with the reserved Parmesan.

PER SERVING 199 kcals, protein 12g, carbs 28g, fat 5g, sat fat 2g, fibre 4g, sugar 6g, salt 0.81g

# Chicken & quinoa salad with beetroot yogurt

*Quinoa is a healthy alternative to rice or couscous – and is just as delicious. It's a real superfood, full of protein and with high levels of calcium, iron, fibre and vitamin B.*

**TAKES 55 MINUTES • SERVES 4**

4 chicken thighs, skin on
2 red onions, cut into wedges (keep the
    roots intact)
3 carrots, cut into batons
1 tbsp olive oil
1 lemon, sliced
2 tbsp clear honey
250g/9oz quinoa
140g/5oz vacuum-packed beetroot
    (not in vinegar), finely chopped
5 tbsp Greek-style yogurt
1 garlic clove, crushed
small handful dill, chopped, plus a few
    fronds to garnish

**1** Heat oven to 200C/180C fan/gas 6. Put the chicken thighs, onions and carrots in a roasting tin. Season, drizzle with the oil and nestle lemon slices around. Bake for 30 minutes. Stir everything, drizzle with the honey and bake for another 15 minutes until the chicken is cooked through and tender.
**2** Meanwhile, cook the quinoa according to the pack instructions, then rinse with cold water and drain thoroughly.
**3** Mix the beetroot, yogurt, garlic, dill and some seasoning in a bowl. In a separate bowl, mix the quinoa, the roasted veg and 2 tablespoons of the cooking juices. Pop the chicken thighs and lemon slices on top, then scatter with dill fronds. Serve with a dollop of the beetroot yogurt on the side.

PER SERVING 535 kcals, protein 28g, carbs 57g, fat 19g, sat fat 5g, fibre 10g, sugar 21g, salt 0.4g

# Courgette caponata with thyme & garlic chicken

*Lots of crusty bread and a glass of Italian red is all the accompaniment this summery Sicilian dish needs.*

**TAKES 35 MINUTES • SERVES 4**

4 garlic cloves, thinly sliced
few thyme sprigs, leaves picked
2 tbsp olive oil
2 red onions, finely sliced
3 celery sticks, thickly sliced on the
    diagonal
4 courgettes, halved lengthways and
    cut into chunks on the diagonal
400g can chopped tomatoes
2 tsp capers
1 tbsp red wine vinegar
3 tbsp sultanas
4 boneless skinless chicken breasts

**1** Put one-quarter of the garlic, the thyme and some seasoning in a bowl with 2 teaspoons of the olive oil and set aside.

**2** Heat the remaining oil in a pan. Tip in the onions and celery, and cook for around 10 minutes until soft. Add the courgettes and the rest of the garlic, and fry for a few minutes to soften. Add the tomatoes, half a can of water, capers, vinegar, sultanas and some seasoning. Gently simmer for about 20 minutes until the juices have thickened and the vegetables are tender.

**3** Meanwhile, cut the chicken breasts in half to open up like a book. Put them between two layers of baking parchment and flatten a little by bashing gently. Heat a griddle pan and rub the chicken with your flavoured oil. Cook for about 3 minutes each side, or until cooked through – you may have to do this in batches. Cut the chicken into strips and serve alongside the courgette caponata.

PER SERVING 276 kcals, protein 34g, carbs 18g, fat 8g, sat fat 1g, fibre 4g, sugar 15g, salt 0.4g

# Bang-bang chicken cups

*As well as making a great starter you could double the recipe and serve the cups as a canapé for a larger gathering.*

**TAKES 35 MINUTES • SERVES 4**

100g/4oz smooth peanut butter
140g/5oz full-fat coconut yogurt or
 natural yogurt mixed with 2 tbsp
 desiccated coconut
2 tsp sweet chilli sauce
2 tsp soy sauce
2–3 spring onions, finely shredded
3 cooked boneless skinless chicken
 breasts, shredded
2 Baby Gem lettuces, big leaves
 separated
½ cucumber, halved lengthways, seeds
 scraped out with a teaspoon, cut
 into matchsticks
toasted sesame seeds, for sprinkling

**1** In your smallest pan, gently warm the peanut butter, yogurt, 3 tablespoons water, sweet chilli and soy sauces until melted together into a smooth sauce. Set aside and allow to cool.

**2** Mix the spring onions and chicken into the sauce and season. You can make this ahead and chill the sauce until needed – if you've cut up the salad ingredients, keep the lettuce leaves and cucumber under damp kitchen paper.

**3** To assemble, add a bundle of cucumber to each lettuce-leaf cup, plus a spoon of the chicken mixture. Sprinkle with sesame seeds and sit on a big platter for everyone to dig in. Or simply serve a pile of lettuce leaves alongside bowls of chicken and cucumber for everyone to make their own.

PER SERVING 176 kcals, protein 16g, carbs 6g, fat 10g, sat fat 3g, fibre 1g, sugar 5g, salt 0.2g

# Barbecued spicy yogurt chicken

*If you want to cook this low-fat chicken indoors, heat oven to 200C/180C fan/gas 6*
*and roast the drumsticks for 30 minutes until the chicken is cooked through.*

**TAKES 30 MINUTES, PLUS**
**MARINATING ● SERVES 4**

8 skinless chicken drumsticks
140g pot natural yogurt
1 tsp chilli powder
1 tbsp ground cumin
1 tbsp ground coriander
2 tsp turmeric powder

**1** With a sharp knife, make a few slashes
in each drumstick. Mix the remaining
ingredients in a bowl and season to
taste. Add the drumsticks to the mix,
rubbing the mixture well into the meat.
If you have time, cover and chill for
30 minutes.
**2** Remove the drumsticks from the
marinade, shaking off the excess.
Cook them on the barbecue for
20–25 minutes, turning occasionally,
until cooked through.

PER SERVING 229 kcals, protein 37g, carbs 6g,
fat 7g, sat fat 2g, fibre none, sugar 2g, salt 0.49g

# Chicken-noodle laksa

*What could be more convivial than a big pan of steaming noodle broth placed in the middle of the table for everyone to help themselves to?*

**TAKES 1 HOUR 10 MINUTES**
- **SERVES 6**

1 medium chicken, jointed into pieces
    and skinned
1 tbsp coriander seeds
3cm/1¼in piece ginger, sliced
2 lemongrass stalks, crushed
zest and juice 1 lime
2 tbsp Thai fish sauce
1 tbsp low-salt soy sauce
200ml/7fl oz light coconut milk
3 garlic cloves, sliced
3 red chillies, deseeded and sliced
handful coriander, chopped (leaves and
    stalks kept separate)
bunch spring onions, sliced
300g/10oz cooked rice noodles
handful mint leaves, chopped
1 tbsp sesame oil (optional)

**1** Put the chicken in a large pan with the coriander seeds, ginger, lemongrass, lime zest and a little salt. Cover with cold water, slowly bring to the boil, then reduce to a simmer for 40 minutes until the chicken falls away from the bone.
**2** Lift the chicken on to a plate and cover with foil. Leave the stock to stand for 10 minutes, skim off any fat and strain into a clean pan. Pull the chicken from the bones and tear into chunks.
**3** Bring the stock back to the boil, then add the fish sauce, soy, coconut milk, garlic, chillies and coriander stalks. Simmer for 2 minutes, return the chicken to the pan and cook for a further 5 minutes until warm. Add the spring onions and lime juice to taste.
**4** Divide the noodles, chicken and veg among six bowls. Season the stock and pour over. Scatter with coriander and mint leaves, and serve with a drizzle of sesame oil, if you like.

PER SERVING 424 kcals, protein 37g, carbs 38g, fat 14g, sat fat 2g, fibre 3g, sugar 3g, salt 1.5g

# Creamy chicken & mango curry

*Either make this fruity curry for a crowd or for just a few friends and freeze the rest.*

**TAKES 1 HOUR 10 MINUTES**
- **SERVES 6–8**

12 boneless skinless chicken thighs
2 tsp turmeric powder
2 tbsp sunflower oil
2 onions, 1 chopped, 1 quartered
2 large ripe mangoes
6 tbsp good-quality korma paste
100g/4oz ginger, roughly chopped
2 tsp ground cumin
1 tbsp black onion seeds (kalonji or nigella)
400g can light coconut milk
600ml/1 pint chicken stock
few coriander sprigs, to scatter
basmati rice, naan bread, mango chutney, lime pickle, to serve (optional)

**1** Toss the chicken thighs with 1 teaspoon of the turmeric and some salt. Heat the oil in a big frying pan and brown the thighs well on both sides. Remove from the pan. Add the chopped onion to the pan and cook for 5 minutes until softened.

**2** Cut the flesh from one mango. Whizz the korma paste, ginger and quartered onion to a paste in a food processor. Cook gently in the pan until softened.

**3** Stir in the remaining turmeric, the cumin and onion seeds, and turn up the heat for a few minutes. Return the chicken to the pan. Stir in the coconut milk and stock. Simmer, covered, for 20 minutes.

**4** Uncover the pan and cook for another 25–30 minutes until the chicken is tender; add a few drops of water to keep it saucy.

**5** Slice the remaining mango and stir in while you shred the chicken with two forks. Season and serve scattered with the coriander, with basmati rice, naan bread, chutney and lime pickle, if you like.

PER SERVING (6) 384 kcals, protein 41g, carbs 17g, fat 17g, sat fat 6g, fibre 3g, sugar 14g, salt 1.2g

# Thai coconut-crumbed chicken traybake

*Get three of your five-a-day fruit and vegetable quota while enjoying a tasty meal with friends.*

**TAKES 1¼ HOURS ● SERVES 4**

1 butternut squash, peeled, deseeded
    and cubed
1 large aubergine, cubed
1 tbsp rapeseed oil
3 tbsp desiccated coconut
4 tbsp fresh breadcrumbs
4 boneless skinless chicken breasts
1 egg, beaten
300g/10oz cherry tomatoes
2 tbsp Thai red curry paste
handful coriander leaves, roughly
    chopped
lime wedges, to garnish

**1** Heat oven to 200C/180C fan/gas 6. In a large, shallow roasting tin, toss the squash and aubergine in the oil, then season and spread out in a single layer. Roast for 30 minutes, turning once.

**2** On a plate, mix the coconut and breadcrumbs with some seasoning. Dip the chicken breasts in the egg, then press in the crumbs to coat, shaking off any excess.

**3** Toss the tomatoes and curry paste in with the roasted veg and give everything a good stir. Nestle the chicken breasts in the veg and pop back in the oven for a further 25–30 minutes until the chicken is cooked through, shaking the pan once or twice. Sprinkle over the coriander and serve with lime wedges to squeeze over.

PER SERVING 414 kcals, protein 38g, carbs 32g, fat 15g, sat fat 7g, fibre 8g, sugar 14g, salt 0.9g

# Italian chicken with soft cheese & spinach

*The topping for the chicken breasts stops them from drying out in the oven.*

**TAKES 1 HOUR ● SERVES 4**

1 large onion, halved and thinly sliced
550g/1lb 4oz scrubbed medium
    potatoes, thinly sliced
4 garlic cloves, sliced
8 pitted Kalamata olives, chopped
1 tbsp rapeseed or olive oil
big salad, to serve

**FOR THE CHICKEN**

85g/3oz low-fat soft cheese
200g/7oz frozen spinach, thawed,
    squeezed really well and chopped
generous grating nutmeg
4 skinless chicken breast fillets
4 stems cherry tomatoes on the vine
    (5–6 tomatoes per stem)

**1** Heat oven to 220C/200C fan/gas 7 and line a large baking sheet with baking parchment. Put the onion slices in a bowl and pour over boiling water to cover them. Leave to soften for 15 minutes. Meanwhile, beat the cheese, spinach and nutmeg together with plenty of black pepper. Spread over the chicken breasts then top with the tomatoes.

**2** Drain the onion slices then toss them with the potato, garlic, olives, oil and some black pepper. Arrange the potato mixture on the parchment in four spaced-apart piles, then flatten. Bake for 25 minutes until almost tender and starting to colour.

**3** Remove from the oven and put a chicken breast and tomatoes on each pile of potatoes then bake for 20 minutes until the chicken and potatoes are tender and cooked all the way through and the tomatoes are roasted. Serve with a big salad.

PER SERVING 352 kcals, protein 39g, carbs 32g, fat 8g, sat fat 2g, fibre 7g, sugar 8g, salt 0.6g

# Saffron rice with chicken & peppers

*Saffron is famously expensive but a little goes a long way, and it gives rice dishes like this a beautiful yellow colour as well as a unique flavour.*

**TAKES 1¼ HOURS ● SERVES 4**

generous pinch saffron
2 tbsp olive oil
4 boneless skinless chicken breasts, each cut into chunks
2 thyme sprigs, leaves stripped
2 medium onions, sliced
3 large garlic cloves, finely chopped
juice 1 lime
1 red pepper, deseeded and cut into strips
100ml/3½fl oz dry white wine
125ml/4fl oz light chicken stock
250g/9oz basmati rice
100g/4oz frozen peas (or fresh, cooked)

**1** Put the saffron and 6 tablespoons warm water in a bowl. Bruise the strands with the back of a teaspoon, and set aside.
**2** Heat the olive oil in a large, weighty casserole dish, then tip in the chicken. Stir-fry for a minute or two over a high heat to seal in the juices, then set aside.
**3** Add the thyme sprigs, onions and garlic to the dish. Fry until golden then pour in the lime juice. Turn down the heat, add the pepper and cook for another 5 minutes. Add the wine, stock and some seasoning. Return the chicken to the pan and simmer for 6 minutes.
**4** Cook the rice in a pan of fast boiling water until tender. Drain and rinse. Heap over the chicken. Drizzle with the saffron and its soaking liquid, and scatter over the peas. Don't stir, but cover and cook for 3 minutes on a low heat until the rice is fluffy. To serve, mix the peas into the rice with the chicken and peppers.

PER SERVING 493 kcals, protein 44g, carbs 61g, fat 8g, sat fat 1g, fibre 3g, sugar none, salt 0.6g

# Moroccan-style chicken with lentils

*This heart-healthy dish could also be cooked in a third of the time in a pressure cooker, if you have one.*

**TAKES 2 HOURS • SERVES 4**

2 tbsp olive oil
8 skinless boneless chicken thighs
2 garlic cloves, crushed
1 tbsp ground cumin
1 tbsp ground coriander seeds
1 tbsp sweet paprika
1 large onion, finely sliced
50g/2oz red split lentils
400g can chopped tomatoes
1 tbsp tomato ketchup
700ml/1¼ pints chicken stock
1 cinnamon stick
200g/7oz whole dried apricots
handful mint leaves, to scatter
(optional)
couscous or rice, to serve

**1** Heat oven to 180C/160C fan/gas 4. Rub 1 tablespoon of the olive oil into the chicken. Mix the garlic, cumin, coriander and paprika together, then rub all over the chicken on both sides.

**2** Heat a large flameproof casserole, add the chicken and cook over a medium heat for 5 minutes until golden on both sides. You might need to do this in two batches, depending on the size of the casserole. Set the chicken aside. Turn down the heat, add the remaining oil and fry the onion for 5 minutes until softened.

**3** Stir in the rest of the ingredients, apart from the mint, and bring to the boil. Put the chicken on top and pour in any juices. Cover and cook for 1½ hours, until the meat is tender and the sauce thickened. Can be cooled and frozen at this stage for up to 1 month. Defrost thoroughly in the fridge, then gently warm through. Scatter with fresh mint leaves, if using, and serve with couscous or rice.

PER SERVING 461 kcals, protein 48g, carbs 40g, fat 13g, sat fat 3g, fibre 6g, sugar 1g, salt 1.45g

# Stuffed-marrow bake

*If you're entertaining on a budget then try to make more of marrows with this cheap but filling main course – add extra bits like chopped olives or chillies, if you want.*

**TAKES 1 HOUR • SERVES 6**

1 tbsp olive oil
1 onion, chopped
1 garlic clove, crushed
1 tbsp dried mixed herbs
500g/1lb 2oz minced chicken
2 x 400g cans chopped tomatoes
1 marrow, cut into 5cm/2in-thick slices
    and centre removed
4 tbsp breadcrumbs
3 tbsp grated Parmesan

**1** Heat oven to 200C/180C fan/gas 6. Heat the oil in a large frying pan and cook the onion, garlic and 2 teaspoons of the herbs for 3 minutes until starting to soften. Add the chicken and brown all over, then tip in the tomatoes and cook for 5 minutes more.

**2** Arrange the marrow slices in a baking dish. Spoon the mince into the middle of each marrow slice, then spoon the rest over the top. Cover with foil and bake for 30 minutes.

**3** Meanwhile, mix the remaining herbs with the breadcrumbs and Parmesan. Remove the marrow from the oven, uncover, and sprinkle over the crumbs. Return to the oven for 10 minutes more until the crumbs are golden and crisp and the marrow is tender.

PER SERVING 198 kcals, protein 24g, carbs 15g, fat 5g, sat fat 2g, fibre 3g, sugar 8g, salt 0.55g

# Chicken-tikka skewers

*Packed with flavour but low in calories, these skewers can be cooked on the barbecue, under the grill or in a griddle pan – whatever's easiest for you.*

**TAKES 40 MINUTES, PLUS MARINATING • SERVES 4**

150g pot low-fat natural yogurt
2 tbsp tikka masala paste
4 boneless skinless chicken breasts, cubed
250g pack cherry tomatoes
4 wholemeal chapatis, warmed, to serve

**FOR THE CUCUMBER SALAD**

½ cucumber, halved lengthways, deseeded and sliced
1 red onion, thinly sliced
handful chopped coriander leaves
juice 1 lemon
50g pack lamb's lettuce or pea shoots

**1** Put 8 wooden skewers in a bowl of water to soak. Mix the yogurt and curry paste together in a bowl, then add the chicken (if you have time, marinate in the fridge for an hour or so).

**2** In a large bowl, toss together the cucumber, red onion, coriander and lemon juice for the salad. Chill until ready to serve.

**3** Shake off any excess marinade, then thread the chicken pieces and cherry tomatoes on to the pre-soaked skewers. Cook under a medium grill for 15–20 minutes, turning from time to time, until cooked through and nicely browned.

**4** Stir the lettuce or pea shoots into the salad, then divide among four plates. Top each serving with two chicken tikka skewers and serve with the warm chapatis.

PER SERVING 214 kcals, protein 37g, carbs 8g, fat 4g, sat fat 1g, fibre 1g, sugar 7g, salt 0.61g

# Cajun chicken with pineapple salsa

*Simple to make but still impressive; you won't need any accompaniments as it's a complete meal.*

**TAKES 40 MINUTES • SERVES 4**

1 red onion, finely chopped
1 tbsp sunflower oil
1 red pepper, deseeded and diced
200g/7oz basmati rice
450ml/16fl oz chicken stock
400g can kidney beans, drained and rinsed
4 boneless skinless chicken breasts
2 tsp Cajun spice mix
140g/5oz fresh pineapple (or 220g can pineapple rings, drained)
½ green chilli, finely chopped
juice 1 lime

**1** Reserve 2 tablespoons of the onion for the salsa. Heat the oil in a pan and cook the remaining onion and half the pepper for 4 minutes or until softened and coloured. Stir in the rice, then pour in the stock. Add the kidney beans and a pinch of salt. Bring to the boil, stir once, cover the pan, then reduce the heat to a gentle simmer. Cook for 15 minutes until the rice is tender and the liquid absorbed.

**2** Cut a slit into each of the chicken breasts, open them up and bash them so they're flat. Season the chicken with the Cajun spice mix and griddle or fry in a non-stick pan for about 4–6 minutes on each side until cooked through. Cut the pineapple into small pieces and mix together with the reserved red onion, the rest of the pepper, the green chilli and lime juice. Spoon some salsa over each chicken breast and serve with the rice.

PER SERVING 451 kcals, protein 42g, carbs 54g, fat 5g, sat fat 1g, fibre 6g, sugar 10g, salt 0.9g

# Herbed chicken, peach & feta salad

*This vibrant main-meal salad makes a great lunch in the garden.*

**TAKES 20 MINUTES • SERVES 4**

200ml/7fl oz vegetable stock, made
   with freshly boiled water
120g/4½oz bulghar wheat
meat from a 900g/2lb ready-roasted
   smoked or unsmoked whole chicken
   (or about 550g/1lb 4oz ready roasted
   chicken breasts), not too fridge-cold
2 ripe yellow-fleshed peaches
25g pack mint
25g pack dill
handful basil (optional)
50g/2oz toasted pecan nut halves,
   some broken, some left whole
85g/3oz feta, crumbled
your favourite dressing, to drizzle

**1** Pour the boiling-hot stock over the bulghar in a large bowl. Cover with cling film and set aside for 15–20 minutes until the stock has been totally absorbed and the grains are tender.
**2** Meanwhile, slice or tear the chicken into bite-size pieces and cut each peach into 12 wedges.
**3** When the bulghar looks dry and has swollen up in the bowl, remove the cling film. Fluff it up with a fork and let cool.
**4** Roughly chop the herbs just before serving, then toss into the bulghar. Spread the herby bulghar over a large platter, then top with the chicken, peaches, pecans and feta. Roughly toss everything together a little and drizzle over the dressing to serve.

PER SERVING 460 kcals, protein 46g, carbs 27g, fat 18g, sat fat 5g, fibre 2g, sugar 4g, salt 1g

# Thai chicken burgers with sweet-potato fries

*Give burger and fries a complete makeover with this altogether healthier and more flavour-packed version.*

**TAKES 50 MINUTES • SERVES 4**

4 sweet potatoes, unpeeled and cut into chunky chips
1 tbsp olive oil
400–500g/14oz–1lb 2oz minced chicken or turkey
2 tbsp Thai red curry paste
6 spring onions, chopped
small pack coriander, chopped
200g/7oz pineapple chunks, diced
juice ½ lime
1 red chilli, deseeded and finely chopped
2 tbsp sweet chilli sauce, plus extra for dipping
1 Little Gem lettuce and 4 toasted burger buns, to serve

**1** Heat oven to 200C/180C fan/gas 6. Toss the sweet-potato chips with the oil and some seasoning on a baking sheet. Roast for 40–45 minutes until golden and crisp.
**2** Mix the mince with the curry paste, half the spring onions, half the coriander and some seasoning. Shape into four burgers.
**3** Mix the remaining spring onions and coriander with the pineapple, lime juice, red chilli and sweet chilli sauce.
**4** When the chips have 10 minutes to go, heat a non-stick frying pan or griddle and cook the burgers for 5 minutes on each side until golden and cooked through. Serve the burgers in the buns with lettuce leaves and salsa piled on top, and the sweet-potato chips and extra chilli sauce in bowls alongside for dipping.

PER SERVING 428 kcals, protein 34g, carbs 57g, fat 8g, sat fat 1g, fibre 7g, sugar 17g, salt 2g

# Mexican chicken stew

*Turn this into a superhealthy feast by serving it with brown rice flavoured with lime and coriander and a big bowl of guacamole.*

**TAKES 1 HOUR • SERVES 5**

1 tbsp olive oil

1 onion, sliced

2 red peppers, deseeded and chopped into large chunks

3 tbsp chipotle paste

2 x 400g cans chopped tomatoes

4 boneless skinless chicken breasts

140g/5oz long grain rice

400g can pinto beans, drained and rinsed

small bunch coriander, most chopped, a few leaves left whole

juice 1 lime

1 tbsp sugar

natural yogurt, to serve

**1** Heat the oil in a deep frying pan and fry the onion and peppers for a few minutes until softened. Stir in the chipotle paste for 1 minute, followed by the tomatoes. Add the chicken breasts, with up to a tomato can-full of water to cover them, and gently simmer, turning occasionally, for 20 minutes until the chicken is cooked through.

**2** Bring a large pan of water to the boil. Add the rice and cook for 12–15 minutes until tender, or according to the pack instructions, adding the beans for the final minute. Drain well and stir in the chopped coriander and lime juice, then check for seasoning before covering to keep warm.

**3** Lift the chicken out on to a board and shred each breast using two forks. Stir back into the tomato sauce with the sugar and season. Serve with the rice, scattering the stew with some coriander leaves just before dishing up and eating with a dollop of yogurt on the side.

PER SERVING 361 kcals, protein 32g, carbs 45g, fat 5g, sat fat 1g, fibre 6g, sugar 14g, salt 0.8g

# Asian chicken, mandarin & cashew salad

*This deliciously crunchy main-course salad makes clever use of a ready-roasted chicken – just don't tell anyone you didn't roast it yourself!*

**TAKES 25 MINUTES ● SERVES 5**

1 ready-roasted chicken

295g can mandarin segments in juice (not syrup)

1 red onion, thinly sliced

1 red pepper, deseeded and cut into chunks

1 fist-sized chunk red cabbage, shredded

100g/4oz toasted salted cashew nuts

60g bag watercress, rocket & spinach salad

2 tbsp toasted sesame seeds

**FOR THE DRESSING**

1 tbsp sesame oil

4 tbsp mandarin juice from the can

2 tbsp rice wine vinegar

**1** Remove the skin from the chicken and discard, then shred the meat from the bones. Discard the carcass (or freeze for stock or soup another time).

**2** Drain the mandarin segments over a bowl to catch the juice, then whisk together 4 tablespoons of the juice with the sesame oil and vinegar to make the dressing.

**3** Layer the shredded chicken, mandarin segments, red onion, pepper, cabbage, cashews, salad leaves and sesame seeds in a big salad bowl or on a platter. Pour over the dressing, toss to combine then serve.

PER SERVING 445 kcals, protein 42g, carbs 14g, fat 24g, sat fat 6g, fibre 4g, sugar 10g, salt 0.5g

# Light chicken korma

*A mild korma is a great curry to start kids on the road to spicier food, and this version ensures you're also giving them something healthy.*

**TAKES 35 MINUTES ● SERVES 4**

1 onion, chopped

2 garlic cloves, roughly chopped

thumb-size piece ginger, roughly chopped

4 tbsp korma paste

4 skinless boneless chicken breasts, cut into bite-size pieces

50g/2oz ground almonds, plus extra to scatter (optional)

4 tbsp sultanas

400ml/14fl oz chicken stock

¼ tsp golden caster sugar

150g pot 0% fat Greek-style yogurt

small bunch coriander, chopped

steamed brown or white basmati rice, to serve

**1** Put the onion, garlic and ginger in a food processor and whizz to a paste. Tip the paste into a large high-sided frying pan with 3 tablespoons water and cook for 5 minutes. Add the korma paste and cook for a further 2 minutes until aromatic.

**2** Stir the chicken into the sauce, then add the ground almonds, sultanas, stock and sugar. Give everything a good mix, then cover and simmer for 10 minutes or until the chicken is cooked through.

**3** Remove the pan from the heat, stir in the yogurt and some seasoning, then scatter over the coriander and flaked almonds, if using. Serve with brown or white basmati rice.

PER SERVING 376 kcals, protein 40g, carbs 28g, fat 11g, sat fat 1g, fibre 3g, sugar 26g, salt 1.1g

# Cacciatore chicken

*Here's a very simplified version of the Italian classic stew – feel free to add a handful of black olives or a splash of red wine to the sauce, if it takes your fancy.*

**TAKES 1 HOUR • SERVES 4**

1 tsp olive oil
1 onion, sliced
2 garlic cloves, sliced
400g can chopped tomatoes
2 tbsp chopped rosemary leaves
4 boneless skinless chicken breasts
small handful basil leaves
favourite seasonal vegetables, to serve
   (optional)

**1** Heat the oil in a pan and fry the onion and garlic for 8 minutes until softened. Add the tomatoes, rosemary and some seasoning, and simmer gently for 10–15 minutes until thickened.

**2** Heat oven to 180C/160C fan/gas 4. Put the chicken on a baking sheet, top with the sauce and bake for 15–20 minutes until cooked through. Serve scattered with basil alongside your favourite veg, if you like.

PER SERVING 171 kcals, protein 32g, carbs 6g, fat 2g, sat fat 1g, fibre 2g, sugar 4g, salt 0.3g

# Cock-a-leekie soup

*You can buy good-quality stock cubes and concentrates, but for purity of flavour you can't beat making a soup like this from scratch.*

**TAKES 1¾ HOURS • SERVES 6**

1 tbsp vegetable oil
1 medium chicken, jointed into pieces
175g/6oz smoked bacon lardons
2 carrots, chopped
2 celery sticks, chopped
1–2 leeks, washed and cut into thick
    rounds (tops reserved)
splash white wine
2 bay leaves
½ bunch thyme sprigs
15–20 stoned prunes
good-quality bread, to serve

**1** Heat the oil in a large heavy-based pan until hot. Fry the chicken pieces in batches until golden brown, then remove and set aside. Add the bacon, carrots, celery and leek tops, and fry for 5 minutes until it all starts to brown. Pour off any excess fat.

**2** Splash in the wine and boil rapidly, scraping the bottom of the pan. Return the chicken pieces with the herbs and add enough cold water to cover. Slowly bring to the boil, then simmer for 40 minutes until the chicken is tender.

**3** Remove the chicken to a plate, cover with foil and leave to cool slightly. Strain the soup into another pan and discard all the other ingredients. Leave to stand for a few minutes, skimming off any fat that rises. Pull the meat from the chicken bones and tear into large chunks.

**4** Simmer the soup with the chicken, leeks and prunes for another 20–30 minutes. Season and serve with bread.

PER SERVING 337 kcals, protein 36g, carbs 9g, fat 16g, sat fat 5g, fibre 3g, sugar 8g, salt 1.1g

# All-in-one roast chicken & vegetables

*This has to be the easiest roast-dinner recipe ever – the chicken, vegetables and gravy are all made in one pan and a portion counts as two of your five-a-day.*

**TAKES 1½ HOURS • SERVES 4–6, WITH LEFTOVER CHICKEN**

1 whole chicken (about 1.5kg/3lb 5oz)
1 lemon, halved
2 garlic cloves
thyme or rosemary sprig
25g/1oz soft butter
800g/1lb 12oz very small salad potatoes, such as Charlotte, halved if large
350g/12oz small Chantenay carrots, or 3–4 normal carrots cut into chunks
1 tsp olive oil
300ml/½ pint hot chicken stock

**1** Heat oven to 220C/200C fan/gas 7. Sit the chicken in a large roasting tin. Stuff the lemon halves into the cavity with the garlic and herb sprig. Smear the butter all over the chicken.

**2** Scatter the vegetables in an even layer around the chicken and drizzle with oil. Season everything, then put in the oven to roast for 30 minutes. Remove from the oven and give the vegetables a stir, reduce the heat to 200C/180C fan/gas 6, then return the chicken to the oven for 50 minutes more.

**3** Remove the chicken from the oven. Pull the leg – if it easily comes away from the body, the chicken is cooked. Scoop the vegetables into a serving dish and keep warm. Using a spoon or a pair of tongs, remove the garlic, lemon and herbs from the chicken and put them in the roasting tin. Squash them down with a potato masher, pour in the chicken stock and soy sauce, stir well and strain into a jug.

PER SERVING (6) 415 kcals, protein 35g, carbs 24g, fat 19g, sat fat 7g, fibre 4g, sugar 5g, salt 0.6g

# Sweet & sour chicken & veg

*Quicker, cheaper and so much healthier than getting a takeaway – the chicken can also be swapped with pork.*

**TAKES 40 MINUTES ● SERVES 4**

425g can pineapple chunks, drained, juice reserved

2 tbsp each tomato ketchup, malt vinegar and cornflour

1 tbsp vegetable oil

1 onion, chopped

1 red chilli, deseeded and sliced

1 red and green pepper, deseeded and chopped

2 carrots, sliced on the diagonal

2 boneless skinless chicken breasts, thinly sliced

125g pack baby corn, sliced lengthways

2 tomatoes, quartered

cooked rice, to serve (optional)

**1** Make the sweet-and-sour sauce by whisking together the pineapple juice, tomato ketchup, malt vinegar and cornflour. There should be 300ml/½ pint – add water or stock if you're short.

**2** Heat the oil in a frying pan or wok over a high heat. Add the onion, chilli, peppers, carrots and chicken, and stir-fry for 3–5 minutes until the vegetables are starting to soften and the chicken is almost cooked.

**3** Add the corn and sauce. Bubble for 2 minutes, add the tomatoes and cook for 2 minutes until the sauce thickens, the chicken is cooked and the vegetables are tender. Serve with rice, if you like.

PER SERVING 230 kcals, protein 20g, carbs 30g, fat 4g, sat fat 1g, fibre 4g, sugar 24g, salt 0.26g

# Chicken-biryani bake

*Get ahead with this double batch of a freezer-friendly healthy twist on the classic curried-rice dish.*

**TAKES 1½ HOURS ● SERVES 8**

1 tbsp olive oil
4 skinless boneless chicken breasts, chopped into chunks
4 skinless boneless chicken thighs, chopped into chunks
2 onions, sliced
4 tbsp curry paste (we used korma and tikka masala)
300g/10oz cauliflower, chopped into small florets
700ml/1¼ pints chicken stock
400g can chopped tomatoes
400g can chickpeas, drained and rinsed
200g/7oz full-fat natural yogurt
300g/10oz spinach leaves
400g/14oz basmati rice, cooked according to the pack instructions
5 tbsp flaked almonds

**1** Heat the oil in a large frying pan. Fry the chicken until browned, then remove and set aside. Gently fry the onions in the residual oil until starting to caramelise, about 10–12 minutes.

**2** Add the paste and cauliflower, stir to coat then return the chicken to the pan. Pour in the stock, tomatoes and chickpeas, and simmer for 30 minutes until the cauliflower is nearly tender. Add a splash more liquid if not everything is covered. Remove from the heat and stir in the yogurt.

**3** Assemble the bake in either one large or two smaller, deep ovenproof dishes. Start with one-third of the spinach leaves, season, then top with one-third of the curry. Finish with one-third of the rice then repeat twice more. Scatter over the almonds. Cool completely if freezing, or heat oven to 220C/200C fan/gas 7 and cook for 20–25 minutes until the topping has crisped and the dish is piping hot.

PER SERVING 463 kcals, protein 40g, carbs 54g, fat 11g, sat fat 2g, fibre 5g, sugar 7g, salt 1.31g

# Chicken Caesar salad

*This salad is normally calorific, but here it's transformed into a superhealthy main course that's rich in calcium and high in vitamin C.*

**TAKES 50 MINUTES ● SERVES 4**

**FOR THE CHICKEN**

1½ tbsp lemon juice, plus extra for squeezing
1 tbsp olive oil
2 tsp thyme leaves, plus a few sprigs
1 garlic clove, bashed to bruise
4 boneless skinless chicken breasts

**FOR THE CROUTONS**

100g/4oz rustic granary bread
2 tbsp olive oil

**FOR THE DRESSING & SALAD**

1 garlic clove, finely chopped
1 tsp Dijon mustard
½ tsp Worcestershire sauce
1 tbsp lemon juice
good pinch chilli flakes
4 anchovy fillets, finely chopped
3 tbsp good-quality mayonnaise
4 tbsp fat-free natural yogurt
1 head cos (or romaine) lettuce, leaves separated
100g bag rocket leaves or watercress
25g/1oz piece Parmesan, shaved

**1** Mix the lemon juice, oil, thyme and garlic in a dish. Add the chicken and coat well. Season and leave for up to 2 hours.

**2** Heat oven to 200C/180C fan/gas 6. Slice the bread into big croutons. Spread them in a single layer on a baking sheet, then brush with the 2 tablespoons oil. Bake for 10 minutes, until golden.

**3** For the dressing, blend the garlic, mustard, Worcestershire sauce, lemon juice, chilli and anchovies until smooth. Add the mayonnaise and yogurt, and blend again.

**4** Heat a griddle pan and add the chicken. Cook for 15–16 minutes, turning twice, until cooked through. Remove, then sit for 5 minutes before slicing.

**5** Tear the larger lettuce leaves into three pieces, leaving the smaller ones whole. Put them all into a large bowl with the rocket or watercress. Coat with half the dressing. Pile on to plates and tuck in the croutons, chicken and Parmesan. Drizzle over the remaining dressing.

PER SERVING 430 kcals, protein 43g, carbs 15g, fat 23g, sat fat 4g, fibre 3g, sugar 4g, salt 1.37g

# Chicken & leek pies with sweet-potato chips

*What filo pastry lacks in butteriness it makes up for in crispness, and it also makes a very good, healthy substitute pie-topping over shortcrust or puff pastry.*

**TAKES 1 HOUR • SERVES 2**

1 large sweet potato, cut into chunky
   chips
4 tsp olive oil
2 boneless skinless chicken breasts,
   chopped into bite-sized chunks
1 leek, finely sliced
1 carrot, chopped
225ml/8fl oz low-sodium chicken stock
2 tsp wholegrain mustard
85g/3oz light soft cheese
2 tbsp chopped tarragon leaves
2 sheets filo pastry

**1** Heat oven to 200C/180C fan/gas 6. In a roasting tin toss the sweet-potato chips with 2 teaspoons of the oil and some seasoning. Cook for 30–40 minutes, until golden and crisp.

**2** Heat 1 teaspoon of the oil in a medium frying pan. Fry the chicken until browned, remove from the pan and set aside. Add the leek and a splash of water, and gently fry until soft, about 7 minutes. Add the carrot and cook for 3 minutes more. Pour in the stock and boil until reduced by half, then add the mustard and soft cheese, stirring well to combine. Return the chicken to the pan, add the tarragon and some seasoning.

**3** Divide the mixture between two small ovenproof dishes. Take the filo sheets and scrunch them up. Top each pie with a sheet and brush with the remaining teaspoon of oil. Cook the pies in the oven with the chips for 15 minutes, until the pastry is golden.

PER SERVING 538 kcals, protein 43g, carbs 55g, fat 17g, sat fat 5g, fibre 7g, sugar 15g, salt 1.4g

# Coronation chicken salad

*Discover a lighter version of this retro salad, which has half the fat of the original but loads more flavour.*

**TAKES 2½ HOURS • SERVES 6**

1.6kg/3lb 8oz free-range organic whole chicken
1 carrot, roughly sliced
4 tarragon sprigs
2 bay leaves
1 tbsp rapeseed oil
1 onion, finely chopped
4 tsp medium curry powder
2 tsp tomato purée
6 soft ready-to-eat apricots, quartered
1 tsp light muscovado sugar
1 tbsp lime juice
100g/4oz mayonnaise
250g/9oz fromage frais
20g pack coriander, leaves only, chopped
1 ripe medium mango, stoned, peeled and sliced
100g bag watercress
6 spring onions, cut into long slivers

**1** Put the chicken in a pan and cover with water. Add the carrot, tarragon and bay leaves, cover then simmer for 1¾ hours then leave to cool. Lift the chicken out and set aside, keeping 200ml/7fl oz of the stock.

**2** Cook the onion in the oil until golden. Stir in the curry powder, reserved chicken stock and the tomato purée, and simmer for 10 minutes. Put the apricots in a pan with water to cover, simmer for 15 minutes. Drain, reserving 1 tablespoon of the liquid. Purée the apricots and liquid. Remove the curry sauce from the heat and add the sugar. Strain then stir in the lime juice and apricot, and cool.

**3** Mix together the mayonnaise and fromage frais, then stir in the curry sauce. Remove the skin from the chicken and strip the meat off the bones. Toss the chicken with the curried sauce, the coriander and most of the mango. Scatter the watercress on to a platter. Spoon the chicken mix on top, tuck in the rest of the mango and finish with spring onions.

PER SERVING 402 kcals, protein 35g, carbs 15g, fat 23g, sat fat 5g, fibre 3g, sugar 14g, salt 0.53g

# Chicken chow mein

*This speedy, kid-friendly supper is a great way of cramming a good variety of vegetables into one meal.*

**TAKES 20 MINUTES • SERVES 4**

3 garlic cloves, crushed

good chunk ginger, grated

1 red chilli, deseeded and chopped

1 tbsp soy sauce

2 tbsp tomato purée

2 boneless skinless chicken breasts, cut into chunky strips

3 blocks dried egg noodles

½ head broccoli, broken into florets

3 carrots, cut into thin sticks

1 tbsp vegetable oil

300g pack beansprouts

3 spring onions, halved and sliced into long strips

1 tbsp oyster sauce

**1** Mix together the garlic, ginger, chilli, soy sauce and tomato purée, then add the chicken and leave to marinate while you prep the rest of the ingredients.

**2** Boil a large pan of water, add the noodles, broccoli and carrots, then cook for 4 minutes before draining.

**3** Heat the vegetable oil in a wok, tip in the chicken and its marinade, then stir-fry for 4–5 minutes until cooked. Toss in the noodles and vegetables, beansprouts and spring onions to warm through, then mix the oyster sauce with 2 tablespoons water and stir in just before serving.

PER SERVING 545 kcals, protein 33g, carbs 80g, fat 12g, sat fat 1g, fibre 7g, sugar 12g, salt 1.98g

# Crispy chicken

*This homemade version of the fast-food takeaway has a lot less fat and a lot more flavour.*

**TAKES 35 MINUTES, PLUS
MARINATING • SERVES 4**

150ml/¼ pint buttermilk
2 plump garlic cloves, crushed
4 skinless boneless chicken breasts
   (about 550g/1lb 4oz in total),
   preferably organic
50g/2oz Japanese panko breadcrumbs
2 tbsp self-raising flour
½ rounded tsp paprika
¼ rounded tsp English mustard powder
¼ rounded tsp dried thyme
¼ tsp hot chilli powder
½ tsp ground black pepper
3 tbsp rapeseed oil

**1** Pour the buttermilk into a wide shallow dish and stir in the garlic. Cut the chicken into slices and coat in the buttermilk mixture. Leave in the fridge for at least 1–2 hours or preferably overnight.
**2** Toast the panko crumbs and flour in a large non-stick pan for 2–3 minutes, stirring regularly, then tip into a bowl and stir in the paprika, mustard, thyme, chilli, pepper and a pinch of sea salt.
**3** Heat oven to 230C/210C fan/gas 8. Line a baking tin with foil and sit a wire rack on top. Transfer half the crumb mix to a food bag. Transfer half the chicken from the buttermilk to the food bag. Seal the bag and shake to cover the chicken.
**4** Heat 1 tablespoon of the oil in a large pan. Add the chicken from the bag and fry for 1½ minutes. Turn the chicken over, add another ½ tablespoon of the oil and fry for 1 minute more. Transfer to the wire rack using tongs. Repeat with the remaining seasoned crumbs, oil and chicken. Bake the chicken on the rack for 15 minutes until cooked and crisp.

PER SERVING 319 kcals, protein 37g, carb 19g, fat 11g, sat fat 1g, fibre 1g, sugar 2g, salt 0.7g

# Chicken burgers

*Chicken burgers get a full healthy makeover – this recipe makes a big batch, perfect for a crowd or if you fancy filling your freezer.*

**TAKES 40 MINUTES • MAKES 8**

2 tbsp olive oil
1 large onion, finely chopped
2 garlic cloves, crushed
85g/3oz porridge oats
450g/1lb minced chicken
100g/4oz dried apricots, finely chopped
1 large carrot, grated
1 egg, beaten
bread rolls and cucumber slices,
   to serve

**1** Heat 1 tablespoon of the oil in a pan and gently fry the onion for 5 minutes until soft. Add the garlic and cook for 1 minute. Add the oats and fry for 2 minutes more. Tip into a bowl and set aside to cool.

**2** Add the rest of the ingredients, apart from the remaining oil, to the cooled mixture and mix well with your hands. Season to taste and shape into eight patties.

**3** Heat oven to 200C/180C fan/gas 6. Heat the remaining olive oil in a large non-stick frying pan and sear the burgers on each side until well coloured (3–4 minutes). Transfer to a baking sheet and cook in the oven for 10–15 minutes. Serve in rolls with the cucumber slices.

PER BURGER 179 kcals, protein 16g, carbs 17g, fat 6g, sat fat 1g, fibre 2g, sugar 9g, salt 0.17g

# Chicken parmigiana

*This dish also works really well with turkey fillets or boneless pork chops – without having to change the method or timings.*

**TAKES 30 MINUTES • SERVES 4**

2 large boneless skinless chicken
    breasts, halved through the middle
2 eggs, beaten
50g/2oz breadcrumbs
50g/2oz Parmesan, grated
1 tbsp olive oil
2 garlic cloves, crushed
½ x 690ml jar passata
1 tsp caster sugar
1 tsp dried oregano
½ x 125g ball light mozzarella, torn

**1** Put the chicken breasts between sheets of cling film and bash out with a rolling pin until they are the thickness of a £1 coin. Dip in the egg, then the breadcrumbs, mixed with half the Parmesan. Set aside on a plate in the fridge while you make the sauce.

**2** Heat the oil and cook the garlic for 1 minute, then tip in the passata, sugar and oregano. Season and simmer for 5–10 minutes.

**3** Heat grill to high and cook the chicken for 5 minutes each side, then remove. Pour the tomato sauce into a shallow ovenproof dish and top with the chicken. Scatter over the mozzarella and remaining Parmesan and grill for 3–4 minutes until the cheese has melted and the sauce is bubbling.

PER SERVING 327 kcals, protein 33g, carbs 22g, fat 13g, sat fat 5g, fibre 1g, sugar 5g, salt 1.31g

# Chicken gumbo

*An authentic Louisiana casserole with creole spices made low fat and packed with okra and other vegetables. Serve with crusty bread or rice.*

**TAKES 1 HOUR • SERVES 4**

1 tbsp olive oil
500g/1lb 2oz skinless boneless chicken thighs, cut into chunks
1 onion, chopped
1 green pepper, deseeded and chopped
3 celery sticks, finely chopped
1 garlic clove, finely chopped
¼ tsp cayenne pepper
1 tsp smoked paprika
1 tsp ground cumin
1 tsp dried thyme
1 bay leaf
1 heaped tbsp plain flour
400g can chopped tomatoes
400ml/14fl oz chicken stock
100g/4oz okra, sliced into 2cm/¾in rounds
small handful sage, leaves chopped

**1** Heat the oil in a large pan with a lid over a medium–high heat. Add the chicken and cook in batches for about 5 minutes to brown all over. Remove the chicken to a plate with a slotted spoon and set aside.

**2** Add the onion, green pepper and celery to the pan, put on the lid and cook for 5 minutes, stirring occasionally until softened a little. Stir in the garlic, spices, thyme and bay leaf, and cook for 1 minute until fragrant.

**3** Return the chicken and any juices to the pan with the flour, stirring to coat everything. Pour in the tomatoes and stock, and bring to the boil, cook for 5 minutes then add the okra and half the sage. Turn down to a simmer, put on the lid and cook for 10 minutes. Then season and serve, scattering over the rest of the sage.

PER SERVING 242 kcals, protein 33g, carbs 12g, fat 7g, sat fat 2g, fibre 4g, sugar 6g, salt 0.7g

# Chicken tikka masala

*Now you can enjoy the nation's favourite curry, without any of the guilt factor, with this lower-fat, freezer-friendly version.*

**TAKES 1 HOUR • SERVES 8**

4 tbsp vegetable oil
4 onions, roughly chopped
6 tbsp chicken tikka masala paste
3 red peppers, deseeded and cut into chunks
8 boneless skinless chicken breasts, cut into 2.5cm/1in cubes
2 x 400g cans chopped tomatoes
4 tbsp tomato purée
2–3 tbsp mango chutney
200g/7oz full-fat natural yogurt
chopped coriander leaves, to scatter
cooked basmati rice and warm naan bread, to serve

**1** Heat the oil and butter in a large, lidded casserole on the hob, then add the onions and a pinch of salt. Cook for 15–20 minutes until soft and golden. Add the paste and peppers, then cook for 5 minutes more to cook out the rawness of the spices.

**2** Add the chicken and stir well to coat in the paste. Cook for 2 minutes, then tip in the tomatoes, purée and 200ml/7fl oz water. Cover with a lid and gently simmer for 15 minutes, stirring occasionally, until the chicken is cooked through.

**3** Remove the lid, stir through the mango chutney and yogurt, then gently warm through. Season, then set aside whatever you want to freeze to cool. Scatter the rest with coriander leaves and serve with basmati rice and naan bread.

PER SERVING 294 kcals, protein 35g, carbs 18g, fat 9g, sat fat 2g, fibre 5g, sugar 16g, salt 1g

# Index

# Also available from BBC Books and *Good Food*